Python Testing with Selenium

Learn to Implement Different Testing Techniques Using the Selenium WebDriver

Sujay Raghavendra

Apress®

Python Testing with Selenium

Sujay Raghavendra
Dharwad, Karnataka, India

ISBN-13 (pbk): 978-1-4842-6248-1
https://doi.org/10.1007/978-1-4842-6249-8

ISBN-13 (electronic): 978-1-4842-6249-8

Managing Director, Apress Media LLC: Welmoed Spahr
Acquisitions Editor: Celestin Suresh John
Development Editor: James Markham
Coordinating Editor: Aditee Mirashi

Cover designed by eStudioCalamar

Cover image designed by Freepik (www.freepik.com)

Distributed to the book trade worldwide by Springer Science+Business Media New York, 1 New York Plaza, Suite 4600, New York, NY 10004-1562, USA. Phone 1-800-SPRINGER, fax (201) 348-4505, e-mail orders-ny@springer-sbm.com, or visit www.springeronline.com. Apress Media, LLC is a California LLC and the sole member (owner) is Springer Science + Business Media Finance Inc (SSBM Finance Inc). SSBM Finance Inc is a **Delaware** corporation.

For information on translations, please e-mail booktranslations@springernature.com; for reprint, paperback, or audio rights, please e-mail bookpermissions@springernature.com.

Apress titles may be purchased in bulk for academic, corporate, or promotional use. eBook versions and licenses are also available for most titles. For more information, reference our Print and eBook Bulk Sales web page at http://www.apress.com/bulk-sales.

Any source code or other supplementary material referenced by the author in this book is available to readers on GitHub via the book's product page, located at www.apress.com/978-1-4842-6248-1. For more detailed information, please visit http://www.apress.com/source-code.

Printed on acid-free paper

To my Baba
Late Raghavendra A S

Table of Contents

About the Author

Sujay Raghavendra works primarily in data science, machine/deep learning, and artificial intelligence. He is currently the Executive Director of Raghavendra Training & Consultancy (RTC), a startup company based in Dharwad, Karnataka, India. He co-founded RTC with Sumedh Raghavendra, his brother, in 2014. He plans and evaluates new technology projects in research and product development. His projects include analyzing a pap smear filter for microscopic medical images, thermal heat sensing in hospitals, OCR for handwritten characters, satellite image analysis, and network automation for maps, forecasting models, text analytics, predictions, and more.

Raghavendra is also a consultant on building research centers for technical universities and colleges. His recent interests include automating test cases through machine learning. He has published numerous research articles in international journals and has been on reviewer committees for various journals and conferences.

About the Technical Reviewer

 **Supreeth Chandrashekhar** is a seasoned software technology professional associated with Philips Healthcare, Bangalore. He has more than eight years of architect experience in building/running highly robust, massively scalable, and extremely secure systems, as well as setting up and managing mid-sized tech teams. He is extremely passionate about building great products that exceed customer expectations.

Acknowledgments

The person behind who I am today is my mother, Mrs. Indumati Raghavendra.

Introduction

This book focuses on how to implement testing techniques using Selenium WebDriver with the Python programming language. This quick reference provides simple, functional test cases with a syntax-based approach for Selenium WebDriver.

You'll begin by reviewing the basics of Selenium WebDriver and its architectural design history. Next, you move on to the configuration and installation of the Selenium library in various web browsers, including the basic commands needed to start test scripts. You'll review keyboard and mouse action commands for testing user interactions on a web page and see how hyperlinks are tested.

The book examines various web elements using the eight different locators provided by Selenium to help you choose the one best suited to your needs. All Python scripts are real ready-to-test examples that are explained thoroughly in problem statements. You'll use different Python design patterns to automate test scripts that can be incorporated with Selenium.

Python Testing with Selenium teaches the expertise to write your own test cases.

CHAPTER 1

Introduction to Selenium

Before Selenium, testing the functionality of a web application was done manually, which took many hours. The testing tended to rely on different scenarios. Each scenario was considered a test case to enact the behavior of the web app before its implementation. These test cases were deployed on various browsers to affirm any issues in the source code.

It requires a dedicated team of testers to check all test cases. Accuracy and time are major constraints in web development, which has led to automated test cases that can be used in different web applications without changing the source code. Selenium was developed to automate test cases.

This first chapter of the book offers a complete overview of Selenium and its core architectural design. The subtopics explain using Selenium and compares it to other testing tools in the domain. Later in the chapter, integrating Python with Selenium is explained. Let's start with a brief history and description of the Selenium tool and the reasons to use it.

What Is Selenium?

Selenium came into existence in 2004 at ThoughtWorks to test a web application named Time and Expenses by Jason Huggins. The tool was developed to test the front-end behavior of an application in various browsers. The tool was popular and open source. The increase in demand for automated testing led to the development of several versions of Selenium over the years, which are discussed next.

Selenium Tools and Versions

ThoughtWorks has released four major versions of Selenium to test web applications. Figure 1-1 shows each version and its release year.

The original version of this chapter was revised. A correction to this chapter is available at
https://doi.org/10.1007/978-1-4842-6249-8_13

S. Raghavendra, *Python Testing with Selenium*, https://doi.org/10.1007/978-1-4842-6249-8_1

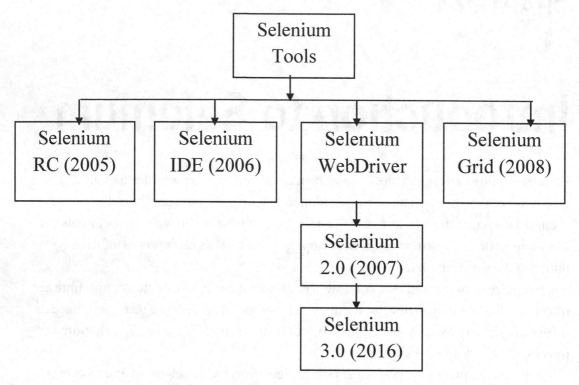

Figure 1-1. *Selenium suite*

Any one (or more) of these Selenium tools can be used by an organization; the choice depends on the test environment's requirements. The first tool developed by ThoughtWorks was Selenium Core in 2004. It allowed the tester to write their own code/ script to automate front-end interactions like keyboard or mouse activities. These activities were similar to a user interacting with the application.

In web application security, there is a policy that grants a test script permission to access data in web pages from the same origin; this policy is called a *same-host* policy. A same-host policy only allows a test case to access pages within the same domain. For example, a test script can access multiple pages within www.apress.com, such as www. apress.com/in/python and www.apress.com/in/about, because of the same-host policy; however, this policy does not allow access to pages from different sites, such as https://google.com or https://wikipedia.org.

Due to the same-host policy, access to code elements is denied or blocked when using external scripts. To avoid this complication, Huggins and Paul Hammant developed a server component that enables you to test a web app with a test script that makes the browser believe that both are from the same source. This core Selenium was eventually known as Driven Selenium or Selenium B.

Selenium RC (Remote Control)

Selenium RC (remote control) was deployed by Dan Fabulich and Nelson Sproul in 2005 to enable a stand-alone server using an HTTP proxy. This solved the issue faced by Selenium Core with the same-host policy. Selenium RC was divided into two parts: Selenium Remote Server and Remote Client. The time it took both the server and the client to receive and send HTTP requests led to the slower execution of test cases; hence, Selenium RC became the least-used tool.

Selenium IDE

In 2006, a completely integrated development environment (IDE) was developed by Shinya Kasatani for testers. It was in the form of a plugin for Mozilla Firefox and Google Chrome web browsers. Selenium IDE used functional tests in a live environment. The feature of this IDE involved tests to record/replay and debug/edit, which was known as Selenium Recorder. The recording scripts were stored in a test script called a Selenese script in Selenium. The test scripts were written in languages like Java, Ruby, JavaScript, and PHP. The IDE also provided data retrieval options for test cases performed for web apps. Selenium IDE is currently actively maintained by Kantu and Katalon.

Selenium Grid

It was difficult to test web applications on the new technologically-enabled devices that were emerging on the market. To solve this issue, in 2008, Philippe Hanrigou at ThoughtWorks developed a grid architecture that allowed you to test apps on any number of remote devices via a browser, which became Selenium Grid. It reduced the time to test scripts on any number of remote devices because it was done in parallel. The test command tests on remote devices via a browser. There are two components necessary to execute a test script on a remote device: a hub/server and a node/remote device.

The hub/server gets requests from the web driver client that allows access and routes it to remote drivers. These drivers are registered on remote devices. A node/remote device has a local OS and browser. The web driver is the part of a browser that performs tests. When defining a script, you need to name a remote device, platform, browser, and so forth, to locate a specific node, and then test scripts are executed for that node.

Selenium WebDriver

Selenium WebDriver is a widely used tool. The advancement in Selenium RC resulted in the development of Selenium WebDriver. The commands in WebDriver are accepted via a client API and are sent to different browsers, such as Mozilla Firefox, Apple Safari, and so forth. Almost all browsers support Selenium WebDriver. Each browser has a specific driver associated with it, which are listed in Table 1-1.

Table 1-1. *Web Browsers and Their respective Selenium WebDriver*

Web Browser	Driver Name
Mozilla Firefox	Firefox (i.e., Gecko)
Google Chrome	Chrome
Apple Safari	Safari
Opera	Opera
Microsoft Internet Explorer	Internet Explorer
Microsoft Edge	Edge

Each driver listed in the table is maintained to support automation for its respective browser. Another browser driver, HTMLUnitDriver, stimulates browsers using a headless browser (HtmlUnit).

Selenium WebDriver allows you to start a web browser directly and manages it by executing commands. To avoid security conflicts and issues, WebDriver uses native OS functionality instead of browser-based JavaScript commands. The Selenium WebDriver version of WebDriver focused on the interface. The later versions are Selenium 2.0 and Selenium 3.0.

Selenium 2.0

In 2007, Simon Stewart at ThoughtWorks created Selenium 2.0, which enables automation on almost all browsers. This version has fewer calls and allows testers/developers to create their own domain-specific language (DSL). The Watir web driver, which is implemented in Ruby, is one of the best examples of DSL.

Selenium 3.0

Developers Simon Stewart and David Burns made a draft to standardize Selenium, which was fully accepted and became a W3C standard protocol in 2019 when it became known as Selenium 3.0.

This completes the overview of Selenium and its evolution through the years; now let's consider the Selenium architecture before diving into the test cases, which are covered in the upcoming chapters of this book.

Selenium WebDriver Architecture

Now that you know about Selenium's various tools and versions, let's look at a tool that helps automate test scripts for a web application. To automate a test script, there is an interaction between the tool and browser that can only be understood by its architecture.

Selenium WebDriver is a tool in the Selenium suite that automates test cases for any web application. The interactions between a web driver tool and the application go through various stages. These stages form an architecture, as depicted in Figure 1-2. The architecture of Selenium WebDriver consists of three main components: Selenium client libraries, browser drivers, and web browsers. The communication among the components is done through a JSON protocol.

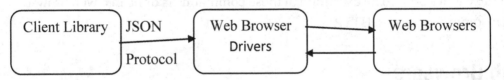

Figure 1-2. Selenium WebDriver architecture

Client Library

A client library is a package of languages supported by Selenium. The core languages supported by Selenium are Python, Java, JavaScript, Ruby, and C# (`https://selenium.dev/downloads/`). Languages like Perl, PHP, GO, DART, R, and Haskell are maintained and developed by a third party (`https://selenium.dev/thirdparty/`). Selenium does not officially support these third-party language bindings.

JSON Wire Protocol

JSON is the acronym for JavaScript Object Notation, which is a lightweight protocol that exchanges data or information from the client to the server and vice versa. JSON is in an easy-to-understand text format, which enabled ThoughtWorks developers to use the JSON wire protocol for communication between the client library and web browser drivers. The server doesn't bother the language used at the client side; it can only read data from the protocol, which is received in JSON format. The JSON wire protocol converts any data or information to JSON format before sending it to the server. It is a REST API.

Note   REST (representational state transfer) defines a set of guidelines to develop an API (application programming interface). One of the rules is to get a server response from the source when linked to a URL.

Web Drivers

Each browser has a web driver associated with it (refer to Table 1-1 for more information). These web drivers are responsible for executing the commands received from the client library. The execution of these commands is done in a web browser, which communicates via HTTP.

Web Browsers

The commands received from an HTTP response from web drivers are executed. Like a client library, core and third-party browsers may be used. The browsers supported by Selenium are Firefox, Internet Explorer, Safari, Opera, Chrome, and Edge. These browsers can be run on any operating system, such as Windows, macOS, or Linux. There are third-party web drivers developed for these web browsers, but they are not recommended.

Why Selenium?

Having examined the Selenium WebDriver architecture, let's further enhance your understanding of Selenium.

Due to the availability of testing tools on the market, a question arises: Why use Selenium for testing? There are several answers to this question, but the primary reason to use Selenium is that it is open source (i.e., freely available to use). The benefits of using Selenium as a testing tool are discussed next.

Open Source

Selenium is open source and can be used at no cost. There is a large community of developers/testers who continuously maintain and support it. You can modify, integrate, or extend Selenium for any testing environment because the code is open source.

Platforms

Selenium WebDriver is cross-platform, which means that it has the flexibility to automate test cases in any operating system, such as Windows, macOS, Unix, and Linux. These test cases written in one OS can be used in any other.

Language Support

Another reason that Selenium has a large community is that it supports multiple programming languages and scripts, like Python, Java, Ruby, Perl, PHP, JavaScript, Groovy, GO, DART, and so forth. This is supported by the Selenium WebDriver language bindings/client library.

Browser

As with platform flexibility, Selenium WebDriver supports almost all browsers. Mozilla Firefox, Google Chrome, Safari, Opera, Internet Explorer, and Edge are supported; they are the most widely used around the globe.

Reuse

Once written, the test scripts can be used as needed across any browser or OS. There are no restrictions on using a test script multiple times.

Easy Implementation

The implementation of Selenium WebDriver depends on the environment and the script used by the developer/tester or organization. This variety is due to the vast number of potential OS and browser combinations. You can develop a customized web driver or framework to implement in a specific testing environment.

Flexible

Refactoring or regrouping in a test script enables you to reduce the amount of code duplication and other complications. Selenium provides developers/testers with this flexibility in a test script.

Hardware Resources

Unlike other testing tools—like UFT, CompleteTest, Katalon Studio, and so forth—Selenium requires fewer hardware resources.

Simulation

Selenium's simulations create the real-time behavior of a mouse and keyboard. This helps to test advanced events like drag, drop, click, hold, scroll, and so forth, with a mouse and similar keypress events made on a keyboard.

The various reasons discussed so far should satisfy reasons to use Selenium as a testing tool but comparing it with the other tools available ensures that Selenium is best at automating tests. This is discussed next.

Other Testing Tools

Now that you know the benefits offered by Selenium, let's now compare Selenium with other testing tools available in the testing domain. This comparison shows precise reasons to use Selenium with Python. The comparison is made on various features of the testing tools. There are four other major testing tools available. Table 1-2 showcases each of these testing tools.

Table 1-2. *Comparing Selenium to Other Testing Tools*

	Selenium	Katalon Studio	UFT (Unified Functional Testing)	TestComplete	Watir
Release Year	2004	2015	1998	1999	2008
Test Platform	Cross	Cross	Windows	Windows	Cross
Test Applications	Web apps	Web/mobile apps, API/web services	Windows/web/ mobile apps, API/web services	Windows/web/ mobile apps, API/web services	Web/mobile apps
Language Support	Python, Java, C#, Perl, JavaScript, Ruby, PHP	Java/Groovy	VBScript	Python, JavaScript, VBScript, Jscript, Delphi, C++, C#	Ruby
Installation Process	Easy to Intermediate (depends on the Selenium tool)	Easy	Easy	Easy	Advanced
Programming Skills	Intermediate to Advanced (for writing desired test cases)	Advanced	Advanced	Advanced	Advanced
Cost	Free	Free	Licensed with maintenance fees	Licensed with maintenance fees	Free
License Type	Open source (Apache2.0)	Freeware	Proprietary	Proprietary	Open source (MIT License)
Product Support	Open source community	Community/ business support	Dedicated staff/ community	Dedicated staff/ community	Open source community

Now that you can see that Selenium is the best-suited automated tool for testing web applications, let's look at why Python is the best language to integrate with Selenium.

Integrating Python with Selenium

Now that Selenium WebDriver

has been discussed, you may want to know which language is used to automate test scripts or cases. Selenium WebDriver supports a variety of languages. The following lists the reasons why Python is the language best suited for testing.

- Python was developed within the scope of the English language, so code syntaxes are easy to read.

- Python scripts are not machine-level code, which makes it easy to code.

- Python offers cross-platform support, which has resulted in a large community of followers.

- The installation of Python on Selenium WebDriver is easier than any other language.

- Python supports the development of web and mobile applications. Python developers can easily migrate to Selenium WebDriver to test their applications because Selenium is supported in Python.

- Selenium provides the Python API that connects straight to the browser. Since Python is less verbose, the Selenium commands are easy to write and execute when connecting to any of the supported browsers.

- The Python programming language is a script; therefore, there is no need for a compiler to convert code from one form to another.

- There is immense library support for Python due to the large number of communities behind it, who maintain and update it regularly. Selenium WebDriver can be extended to build more advanced test cases by automating as per the needs of the organization or individual.

- Python libraries also support different language bindings. This helps to automate test cases for applications developed in other languages.

Listings 1-1 through 1-5 present a simple program for the languages that are supported by Selenium WebDriver. The program opens a browser, visits a specified URL, and searches a query in it. The program first imports the necessary Selenium WebDriver libraries. WebDriver then opens the Mozilla Firefox browser and specifies `www.apress.com` as the URL to visit. Next, it locates the search bar element in the Apress site. After locating the element, this book's title, *Python Testing with Selenium*, is entered as a query in the search bar and submitted. The submitted query provides a new web page with the books associated with the query.

Listings 1-1 through 1-5 illustrate how easy Python is to implement test cases with Selenium web driver when compared to other programming languages, such as Java, C#, Ruby, and PHP.

Listing 1-1. Python Code

```
#Importing selenium libraries in python
from selenium import webdriver

#Opening web Firefox browser using webdriver
driver=webdriver.Firefox()

#Adding URL to open in browser
driver.get("http://www.apress.com")

#Finding Element of search bar
search=driver.find_element_by_name("query")

#Searching book name as string/query in search bar
search.send_keys("Python Testing with Selenium")

#Submit string to search bar
search.submit()

# Close Firefox browser
driver.quit()
```

Listing 1-2. Java Code

```
//Importing Libraries in JAVA
importorg.openqa.selenium.By;
importorg.openqa.selenium.WebDriver;
```

```java
importorg.openqa.selenium.WebElement;
importorg.openqa.selenium.firefox.FirefoxDriver;

public class Search {

public static void main(String[] args) {

        //Opening Firefox Browser
        WebDriver browser = new FirefoxDriver();

        //Opening Apress Website
        browser.get("http://www.apress.com");

        //Finding Element of search bar
        WebElement search =driver.findElement(By.name("query"));

        //Searching book name as query
        search.sendKeys("Python Testing with Selenium");

        //Submitting the query
        search.submit();

        //Closing browser
        browser.close();
}
}
```

Listing 1-3. C# Code

```csharp
//Importing Libraries in C#
using System;
using OpenQA.Selenium;
using OpenQA.Selenium.Firefox;
using OpenQA.Selenium.Support.UI;

class Apress
{
staticvoid Main()
{
    // Opening Browser
    WebDriver browser = newFirefoxDriver();
```

```
    // Visit Apress Site
    browser.Navigate().GoToUrl("http://www.apress.com");

    // Finding Element of search bar by name
    WebElement search = driver.FindElement(By.Name("query"));

    // Search Book name
    search.SendKeys("Python Testing with Selenium");

    // Submit book name
    search.Submit();

    // Submit book name
    browser.Close();
}
}
```

Listing 1-4. Ruby Code

```
//Library Import
require "selenium-webdriver"

// Open Firefox
browser= Selenium::WebDriver.for:firefox

// Visit Apress Site
browser.navigate.to "http://www.apress.com"

// Finding Element of search bar
search=browser.find_element(:name, 'query')

// Search Book name
search.send_keys"Python Testing with Selenium"

// Submit book name
search.submit

//Closing browser
browser.close
```

Listing 1-5. PHP Code

```php
<?php

require_once('vendor/autoload.php');
use Facebook\WebDriver\Remote\RemoteWebDriver;
use Facebook\WebDriver\WebDriverBy;

$web_driver = RemoteWebDriver::create(
    "https://api_key:api_secret@hub.testingbot.com/wd/hub",
        array("platform"=>"WINDOWS", "browserName"=>"chrome", "version" =>
        "latest", "name" => "First Test"), 120000
    );
$web_driver->get("http://apress.com");

$element = $web_driver->findElement(WebDriverBy::name("query"));
if($element) {
$element->sendKeys("Python with Selenium");
$element->submit();
    }
print$web_driver->getTitle();
$web_driver->quit();
?>
```

Summary

This chapter overviewed Selenium WebDriver, including an introduction to its various versions. Emphasis was given to Selenium's architectural design, which provides the complete interaction process necessary to automate the test case. The importance of Selenium was discussed, including its multiple benefits and its distinction over other major testing tools. At the end of the chapter, the significance of Python integration with Selenium was shown in simple test case scenarios using Python and other languages. We further study how integration is done in different environments. Setup and configuration with Python are illustrated in the next chapter.

CHAPTER 2

Getting Started

In the previous chapter, a complete overview of Selenium and its architectural design were discussed, including the significance of integrating Python with Selenium. Let's now dive into integration.

This chapter covers the basic building blocks in writing automated test cases using Selenium with Python. It explains the configuration and the installation of the required tools, including the Selenium library. It also covers the configuration of the Selenium drivers associated with various browsers.

Before writing a test case, you need to know the browser commands for initializing a test case, which are illustrated in examples in this chapter.

Note A Python script in Selenium is described as a *test case*.

The first half of this chapter is devoted to the installation of the Python programming language, the Selenium package, and the available drivers. The second half of the chapter covers the basic browser commands that are essential to running a test case using the installed web driver. Let's start with the basic Python installation.

Installing Python

First, you need to install Python. If you are new to Python, follow these steps to install it in Windows.

1. Open a browser and go to `https://python.org/downloads/windows/`.

2. Download any release beneath the title **Python Releases for Windows**. (Select a Python version higher than 3.6.0; the latest release version at the time of writing is 3.8.5.)

© Sujay Raghavendra 2021
S. Raghavendra, *Python Testing with Selenium*, https://doi.org/10.1007/978-1-4842-6249-8_2

3. Select the Windows version (Windows x86-64 executable installer for 64-bit or Windows x86 executable installer for 32-bit).

4. Run the Python installer and add the Python path to it.

Note   Python comes preinstalled on Mac and Linux.

Now you can install the Selenium library for Python, which is explained next.

Installing Selenium

Once Python is installed on your system, you can utilize pip to download the Selenium package. The command to install Selenium using pip is

```
pip install selenium
```

The same syntax can be used for other package installations by replacing `selenium` with another package name, which is discussed in another chapter of this book. The Selenium version used in this book is 3.141.0. If a lower version of the Selenium library is already installed, or if you need to upgrade the current version, use the following command.

```
pip install --upgrade selenium
```

The next process, driver installation supported by Selenium, is explained next.

Installing Drivers

A driver is required to interact with the specified browser. Each browser has a particular Selenium WebDriver associated with it, so you need to install any one of the drivers provided; for example, geckodriver is a Selenium WebDriver that only operates with Mozilla Firefox. Table 2-1 lists each driver and its associated installation source.

Table 2-1. *Web Drivers and Installation Sources*

Web Driver	Source
Mozilla Firefox	https://github.com/mozilla/geckodriver/releases
Google Chrome	https://sites.google.com/a/chromium.org/chromedriver/downloads
Microsoft Edge	https://developer.microsoft.com/en-us/microsoft-edge/tools/webdriver/
Apple Safari	https://webkit.org/blog/6900/webdriver-support-in-safari-10/

After the installation of the driver of your choice, you need to learn the basic commands that are associated with the browser. These browser commands are necessary to run any of the test cases explained in the book. Let's look at the various browser commands next.

Browser Commands

Let's now look at how to run a test case in different browsers. This is the first stage in running a test case. Later, each browser command is discussed.

To initialize a test case in Selenium, you need to know the basic browser commands. Opening a specified web browser is mandatory for any test case to take place. The available commands are discussed next.

Opening a Web Browser

Selenium supports multiple web browsers, and each has its own driver. The executable path of the associated driver should be used to open any web browser. The syntax for opening a driver is

```
driver = webdriver.Browser_name(executable_path="driver_path")
```

Mozilla Firefox

Before opening Firefox, you need to import the necessary Selenium libraries. A WebDriver instance should be created to open this browser.

```
#Import Selenium Library
from selenium import webdriver

#Open Mozilla Firefox
driver = webdriver.Firefox(executable_path=r'C:\Driver\path\
\geckodriver.exe')
```

Google Chrome

The Chrome driver needs to be installed before executing any test case in Chrome. You can test in this browser by using the following command.

```
from selenium import webdriver

#Open Google Chrome
driver = webdriver.Chrome(executable_path=r'D:\chromedriver.exe')
```

Microsoft Edge

To test a case in the Microsoft Edge browser, the Edge driver needs to be installed, and then the Selenium WebDriver is used to execute it.

```
from selenium import webdriver

#Open Microsoft Edge
driver = webdriver.Edge(executable_path=r'D:\msedgedriver.exe')
```

Internet Explorer

The path for the Internet Explorer executable is needed to test a case in that browser.

```
#Import Selenium Library
from selenium import webdriver

#Open Internet Explorer
driver = webdriver.Ie(executable_path=r'D:\IEdriverserver.exe')
```

Note   Mozilla Firefox is the most often used web driver in this book.

Closing a Browser

The close() function closes a currently open window using the Selenium driver. It does not affect the other windows that are opened. The execution process remains active.

```
from selenium import webdriver
driver = webdriver.Firefox()

driver.get('https://apress.com')

print("Browser Window opened")

#Close function
driver.close()
print("Browser Window closed")
```

Quit Browser

The quit() function closes all the open windows. It also terminates the execution process of the driver.

```
from selenium import webdriver
driver = webdriver.Firefox()

driver.get('https://google.com')

print("Browser opened")

#Quit function
driver.quit()
print("Terminates process")
```

Opening a Web Page

Testing takes place when the web page is open, and the web elements wrapped in it. A web page can be opened online or offline (i.e., with or without any Internet connection). To open a web page, Selenium uses the get() method, which initializes the page that is to be loaded in a specified browser. There are two ways to open a web page, which are discussed next.

Open a Page Online

HTTP or HTTPS protocols are used to open an online web application or page. The get() method completes the loading of the web page and then transfers the control to the next line of code.

```
from selenium import webdriver
driver = webdriver.Firefox()

#Open web page online
driver.get('https://apress.com')

print("Page opened Online")
```

Open a Page Offline

Opening a page offline is used to test web pages or web applications locally. To perform a test, you need to have the files locally stored on a computer. This works for pages that do not need an Internet connection. You need to provide a file location instead of a URL to open it in a browser.

```
from selenium import webdriver
driver = webdriver.Firefox()

#Open web page offline
driver.get('file:///C:/File/Path/file_name.html')

print("Page opened Offline ")
```

The protocols supported by the get() method to open a web page are described in Table 2-2.

Table 2-2. *Protocols Supported by the get() Method*

Protocols	Description
file	Used for a web page stored locally on a computer
HTTP	Tests a web page hosted on a server
HTTPS	When testing on server there are two different protocols associated with the domain, i.e., HTTP or HTTPS.

When the protocol is mismatched, Selenium throws an exception.

Setting the Browser Size

Most web applications or web pages are developed using responsive frameworks. Responsive web pages adjust according to the browser size. To test pages with different browser sizes, Selenium provides the commands discussed next.

Maximize

The `maximize` function in Selenium maximizes the current web browser. Testers use it to test the responsiveness of a web page. It is used by the browser when it is not opened in a maximized state.

```
from selenium import webdriver

driver = webdriver.Firefox(executable_path=r'C:\Users\ADMIN\Desktop\
geckodriver.exe')

#Open apress webpage
driver.get('https://apress.com')

#Maximise Window
driver.maximize_window()
print("Browser is maximised")
```

When the browser is already in a maximized state, the function does not have any impact on the browser.

Fullscreen

The fullscreen function sets the browser to fullscreen mode. The title, URL, address bar, tabs, and so forth, are not visible on the web page visible when in fullscreen.

```
from selenium import webdriver

driver = webdriver.Firefox()

#Open apress webpage
driver.get('https://apress.com')

#FullScreen
driver.fullscreen_window()
print("Browser is Fullscreen")
```

Setting the Size

This function resizes the browser window size by setting up height and width. The browser is resized to test the responsiveness of a web application/page.

```
from selenium import webdriver

driver = webdriver.Firefox()

#Open apress webpage
driver.get('https://apress.com')

#Set Window Size
driver.set_window_size(500,400)
print("Sets Browser Size")
```

Setting the Browser Position

The set method in Python Selenium sets the browser position along the x and y axes. The position of x and y starts at (0,0) from the top-right corner of the screen.

```
from selenium import webdriver

driver = webdriver.Firefox(executable_path=r'C:\Users\ADMIN\Desktop\
geckodriver.exe')
```

```
#Open apress webpage
driver.get('https://apress.com')
#Set Window Position
driver.set_window_position(x=500,y=400)
print("Sets Browser Position")
```

Setting the Size Using Coordinates

This method sets the browser with position and dimensions. The position concerns the x and y coordinates, whereas dimensions are with height and width.

```
from selenium import webdriver

driver = webdriver.Firefox()

#Open apress webpage
driver.get('https://apress.com')

#Set Window Size with co-ordinates
driver.set_window_rect(x=30, y=30, width=450, height=500)
print("Sets Browser Size with co-ordinates")
```

Getting the Browser Position

In some test cases, the browser position is required to perform actions based on it. The get method returns the position of the browser window with respect to x and y positions in a Python dictionary.

```
from selenium import webdriver

driver = webdriver.Firefox()

#Open apress webpage
driver.get('https://apress.com')

#Get Window Position
window_pos= driver.get_window_position()
print(window_pos)
```

Getting the Window Size

The height and width of the browser window are returned in a Python dictionary when this function is used.

```python
from selenium import webdriver

driver = webdriver.Firefox()

#Open apress webpage
driver.get('https://apress.com')

#Get Window Size
print(driver.get_window_size())
```

Navigation Commands

The navigation commands are related to the browser feature that enables a tester to navigate through the browser history by using the back and forth commands or refresh commands. These commands are supported in Python Selenium.

Back

The back() function is used to navigate to a previously visited page in the same browser tab.

```python
from selenium import webdriver

driver = webdriver.Firefox()

#Open apress webpage
driver.get('https://apress.com')

#Open Google page
driver.get('https://google.com')

#Go back to previous 'apress' page
driver.back()
print("Moved to first page")
```

Forward

This function helps to click on forward button of web browser which eventually goes to next page if available.

```
from selenium import webdriver

driver = webdriver.Firefox(executable_path=r'C:\Users\ADMIN\Desktop\
geckodriver.exe')

#Open apress webpage
driver.get('https://apress.com')

#Open Google page
driver.get('https://google.com')

#Go back to previous 'apress' page
driver.back()
print("Moved to first page")

#Go to current page
driver.forward()
print("Moved to second page")
```

Refresh

The refresh() function reloads the current page in the web browser.

```
from selenium import webdriver
driver = webdriver.Firefox()

#Open apress webpage
driver.get('https://apress.com')

print("Page will be Refreshed")

#Page refresh command
driver.refresh()

print("Page is Refreshed")
```

The traditional way to run a test case is discussed next.

Running a Python Test Case

Let's now run the Python file (i.e., test case). The process of running a test case is done in only a few simple steps.

The following explains how a Python test case file is executed in Windows.

1. Click the Windows button, which is on the bottom left corner of the screen.

2. Enter the **cmd** keyword, which is a shortcut for the Command prompt. Click it.

3. Change the path to a file location where the test case is located using the following command.

   ```
   cd dsktop/selenium
   ```

4. Use the following command to run the test case.

   ```
   python file_name.py
   ```

`.py` is the test case extension for Python Selenium.

Summary

In this chapter, you learned the basic procedure to install Python and its Selenium library. The chapter also explained the installation and implementation of a few web drivers in the context of Selenium. You learned about the initialization of each web driver and some associated browser commands. These basic browser commands become more concrete as you move gradually through the next chapters. At the end of the chapter, you went through a procedural way to run a test case.

The following chapter explains the mouse and keyboard actions that use the same web browser commands.

## CHAPTER 3

Mouse and Keyboard Actions

The previous chapter covered Python installation and configuration with Selenium to automate test cases. The basic web browser commands that are necessary to run a test case in WebDriver were also reviewed. This chapter guides you through all the actions users tend to make with a web application using a mouse and keyboard.

In web applications, web elements are bound to certain actions or events that need to be performed to execute a complete test case. These actions or events, when tested with Selenium action commands, lead to finding bugs related to the user interface.

There are various mouse and keyboard actions that are used by the user/client in a web application. Selenium provides ActionChain, which is a powerful library function to test user behavior on any UI elements on a page. Before performing an action function on a UI element, you need to locate it (see Chapter 4).

Action Chains

ActionChains automate low-level mouse and keyboard interactions in a test case. The interactions are classified by the device (i.e., the mouse or the keyboard), which are further classified on similar events associated with it.

`perform()` is an important function that enables all the actions by the mouse and keyboard to be implemented is performed. All ActionChains functions related to the mouse and keyboard work only when the `perform()` function is used; if it is not used, then the ActionChain function results in no action on a web page.

Multiple actions are aligned in a queue when used for a web element. These actions are performed after the `perform()` function is called. Action is needed before using the `perform()` function (an example of mouse and keyboard actions are demonstrated later). Now let's check some actions associated with the mouse.

© Sujay Raghavendra 2021
S. Raghavendra, *Python Testing with Selenium*, https://doi.org/10.1007/978-1-4842-6249-8_3

Mouse

The mouse can enact operations and actions like click, drag, move, and so forth. These actions are performed with a web element in a web application. For example, the selection of a button, such as a default Submit button, is done by clicking a mouse (see Chapter 6), or a web element is displayed or located after performing this action.

The click may be done by the left or the right mouse button using single or multiple clicks. Selenium in Python offers methods to test actions related to the mouse, which are described next.

Click

click(web_element) is a function in which a web element is selected by pressing the left mouse button. The parameter passed is for one web element that needs to be selected or clicked.

When no parameter (i.e., web element) is passed, the left mouse button is clicked to its present position in the web application.

```
from selenium import webdriver
from selenium.webdriver.common.action_chains import ActionChains

driver = webdriver.Firefox()

driver.get("http://www.apress.com")

# Go to button
web_element=driver.find_element_by_link_text("Apress Access")

#Clicking on the button to be selected
web_element.click()
```

Click and Hold

click_and_hold(web_element) is a method in which a mouse pointer is first moved to a specific web element, and the same element is clicked using the left mouse button. Once clicked, the element is not released, which results in holding it.

In the following example, the middle of an element is clicked and held.

```
from selenium import webdriver
driver=webdriver.Firefox()

# Direct to url
driver.get("http://www.apress.com")

# Locate 'Apress Access' web element button
button=driver.find_element_by_link_text("Apress Access")

# Execute click-and-hold action on the element
webdriver.ActionChains(driver).click_and_hold(button).perform()
```

Context Click

context_click(web_element) is a function that moves the mouse pointer to a specific web element, and then a context click is initiated on that element. A right mouse button click is called a *context click* in ActionChains.

Here's an example.

```
driver.get("http://www.apress.com")

# Go to button
button=driver.find_element_by_link_text("Apress Access")

# Perform context-click
webdriver.ActionChains(driver).context_click(button).perform()
```

If no web element is defined in the context function, then the mouse button is clicked in its present position.

Double Click

double_click(web_element) is a method in which a mouse pointer goes to the located web element, and then the left mouse button is clicked twice (double-clicked).

Here is an example.

```
driver.get("http://www.apress.com")

# Go to button
button=driver.find_element_by_link_text("Apress Access")

# Double click on button
webdriver.ActionChains(driver).double_click(on_element=button).perform()
```

It clicks the current position when no element is specified.

Move to an Element

The move_to_element(web_element) function moves the mouse to a web element. It is mainly focused on drop-down menus, where you can scroll or click after moving the mouse over it.

Here is an example.

```
from selenium import webdriver
from selenium.webdriver.common.action_chains import ActionChains
from selenium.webdriver.support import expected_conditions as EC
from selenium.webdriver.support.ui import WebDriverWait
from selenium.webdriver.common.by import By

driver= webdriver.Firefox(executable_path=r'C:\Users\ADMIN\Desktop\
geckodriver.exe')

driver.get("http://www.apress.com")

main_menu=driver.find_element_by_link_text("CATEGORIES")
ActionChains(driver)\
        .move_to_element(main_menu)\
        .perform()

# Wait for sub menu to be displayed
WebDriverWait(driver, 3).until(EC.visibility_of_element_located
((By.LINK_TEXT, "Python")))

sub_menu=driver.find_element_by_link_text("Python")
sub_menu.click()
```

(There are a few other library imports besides ActionChains—which are discussed in future chapters—that pertain to exceptions and waits.) The program moves the mouse pointer to the Categories link in the main menu and waits for three seconds to jump to the Python submenu.

Move Offset

The mouse moves to the specified x and y offset from its current position. The x and y offset values in the function is an integer and can be positive or negative. The following is the syntax.

move_by_offset(xoffset, yoffset)
```
driver.get("http://www.apress.com")

#Offset positions of x and y
x =268
y =66

#Move element with offset position defined
webdriver.ActionChains(driver).move_by_offset(x,y).perform()
```

When the specified coordinates are beyond the web page window, then the mouse moves outside the window. The default coordinates of offset are (0, 0).

The following syntax reflects moving a mouse with specified coordinates. Here the mouse moves with respect to element positions. The earlier method had mouse movements covering the whole screen as a frame.

```
move_to_element_with_offset(to_element, xoffset, yoffset)
```

The offset values start from the top-left corner of any specified web element. The value is an integer that can be positive or negative. A negative xoffset value indicates the left side of the specified web element. Similarly, a negative value in yoffset indicates the upward side of the web element. The following is an example of this function.

```
driver.get("https://www.apress.com/")
# get  element
element = driver.find_element_by_link_text("CATEGORIES")
# create action chain object
action = ActionChains(driver)
```

```
# perform the operation
action.move_to_element_with_offset(element, 200, 50).click().perform()
```

The offset positions can be used when a web element is statically placed on a web page and cannot be used for relative positions.

Drag and Drop

drag_and_drop() drags a source element to a specified or target location. A source element is the web element that needs to be dragged to the target location.

The following is HTML code for drag-and-drop elements.

```
<html>
<head>
<style type="text/css">
#drag,#drop {
float:left;padding:15px;margin:15px;-moz-user-select:none;
        }
#drag{ background-color:#A9A9A9; height:50px; width:50px;
border-radius:50%;      }
#drop{ background-color:#fd8166; height:100px; width:100px;
border-radius:50%;  }
</style>
<script type="text/javascript">
function dragStart(ev) {

ev.dataTransfer.setData("Text", ev.target.getAttribute('id'));

ev.dataTransfer.effectAllowed='move';
ev.dataTransfer.setDragImage(ev.target,0,0);
return true;
        }
function dragEnter(ev) {
event.preventDefault();
return true;
        }
```

```
function dragOver(ev) {
return false;
          }
function dragDrop(ev) {
var src=ev.dataTransfer.getData("Text");
ev.target.appendChild(document.getElementById(src));
ev.stopPropagation();
return false;
          }
</script>
</head>
<body>

<h1>Drag and Drop</h1>
<center>
<div id="drop" ondragenter="return dragEnter(event)" ondrop="return
dragDrop(event)" ondragover="return dragOver(event)">Drop here</div>

<div id="drag" draggable="true" ondragstart="return dragStart(event)">
<p>Drag</p>
</div>
</center>
</body>
</html>
```

There are two circles defined for these two elements, in which one element can drag a smaller circle to drop onto the larger one. This is a simple example of drag-and-drop elements. On a web page, the drag-and-drop function is commonly used to move an image slider or files to a specific area that is uploaded.

The following is the Selenium code to drag and drop the circle shown in Figure 3-1.

```
from selenium import webdriver
driver=webdriver.Chrome()

# Navigate to page stored as local file
driver.get("drag_and_drop.html")

# Locate 'drag' element as source
element1 =driver.find_element_by_id("drag")
```

```
# Locate 'drop' element as target
element2  =driver.find_element_by_id("drop")
# Perform drag and drop action from
webdriver.ActionChains(driver).drag_and_drop(element1,element2).perform()
```

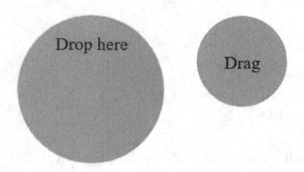

Figure 3-1. *Drag and drop*

Drag and Drop By

With drag_and_drop_by(source, x_offset, y_offset), the left mouse button is held until it moves the web element to the defined offset values of x and y, respectively, and then the button is released. A web element is a source element in the given syntax.

Here's an example.

```
driver.get("drag_and_drop.html")

#Locate circle1 element
circle1 =driver.find_element_by_id("drag")
#Locate circle2 element
circle2  =driver.find_element_by_id("drop")

#Getting offset values
x_off=circle2.location.get("x")
y_off=circle2.location.get("y")
```

```
#PerformdragAndDropBy to circle2 element
webdriver.ActionChains(driver).drag_and_drop_by_offset(circle1, x_off,
y_off).perform()
```

Note   Due to a compatibility issue between Firefox and Selenium, the drag-and-drop function used with plain JavaScript may not work.

Release

The release() function frees the clicked left mouse button. It is most effective for web elements relating to drag and drop. If no web element is passed, then the mouse button is released in its current position on a web page.

Here is an example.

```
driver.get("drag_and_drop.html")

#Locate circle1 element
circle1 =driver.find_element_by_id("drag")
#Locate circle2 element
circle2   =driver.find_element_by_id("drop")

#Release action after performing necessary actions
ActionChains(driver)
        .click_and_hold(circle1)
        .move_to_element(circle2)
        .perform()
        .release()
        .perform()
```

Now that we've reviewed all the mouse actions from ActionChains in Selenium, let's now look at keyboard actions.

Keyboard Actions

Keyboard actions are also necessary for interacting with a web application. Four primary actions are associated with the keyboard. These actions are discussed next.

Key Down

The key_down(value, web_element) function works with the press of a key. It is mainly used with modifier keys, such as Shift, Control, Alt, and so forth.

Key Up

The key_up(value, web_element) function releases the modifier key pressed. It is usually used after the key down method.

Send Keys

The send_keys_to_element(send_keys) method sends keypresses from the keyboard to the currently selected web element. It can be used for a single key or multiple keys.

Most of the time, keyboard actions are used together. The following is a brief example of keyboard actions that select and copy text from a web page.

```
#Import necessary libraries
from selenium import webdriver
from selenium.webdriver.common.keys import Keys
from selenium.webdriver.common.action_chains import ActionChains

driver=webdriver.Chrome()

driver.get('https://en.wikipedia.org/wiki/Apress')

ActionChains(driver)\
        .key_down(Keys.CONTROL)\
        .send_keys("a")\
        .key_up(Keys.CONTROL)\
        .key_down(Keys.CONTROL)\
        .send_keys("c")\
        .key_up(Keys.CONTROL)\
        .perform()
```

In the code, you see that all the contents of the web page were selected and copied using keyboard actions that are available in Selenium.

Send Keys to Element

In `send_keys_to_element(web_element, send_keys)`, the keys are sent to the web element in the given function, which makes it different from the send keys function that sends only the keys, because there is no element mentioned in it.

Mouse and keyboard actions can be combined to use for one or multiple web elements on a web page.

Pause

In `pause(secs)`, the actions are delayed (paused) for a specified duration of time (in seconds). It displays a web element before performing actions.

Reset

The `reset_actions()` function clears or removes all the stored actions that are associated with a web element. The actions can be stored locally or on the remote end.

Summary

This chapter focused on the mouse and keyboard actions that a user performs to interact with a web page. The chapter starts with all the mouse actions that are supported in Selenium. Then, various actions and their corresponding examples are demonstrated. Later, you learned the four main keyboard functions available to a user.

Before applying these actions, you need to locate the element. The task to locate web elements is done by web locators in Selenium, which is discussed in the next chapter.

CHAPTER 4

Web Elements

You learned about the basic actions of the mouse and keyboard in the previous chapter. Now you need to locate a web element to perform these actions. This chapter explains how a web element can be located. There are several types of web elements that are used to build web applications. To test a web application, you first need to trace the web elements in it. The elements can be anywhere on a web page. These web elements can be located or traced by locators provided by Selenium WebDriver.

Locators find the web elements in a web application; hence, the entire chapter is dedicated to web elements and locators. Locators with built-in functions are also demonstrated in a test case. Before diving into a web locator and its types, let's start with learning what web elements are.

Elements/Web Elements

Elements are generally defined as anything between the start and end HTML tags. A web page or application is formed from many different elements. These elements, which are used multiple times in a web application, are called *web elements*.

Note The terms *elements* and *web elements* are used interchangeably.

To avoid confusion among multiple web elements that serve the same purpose, they are distinguished by using unique attributes. The defined attribute has a corresponding name, which should be unique, which serves as a unique property for the web element. This attribute helps the locator.

Note Web elements can be situated anywhere on the page.

© Sujay Raghavendra 2021
S. Raghavendra, *Python Testing with Selenium*, https://doi.org/10.1007/978-1-4842-6249-8_4

Now you have a basic understanding of web elements. To identify the web elements available on a web page, you need to know about locators. Since each web element is different, there are different web locators, which are discussed next.

Web Locators

At least one web element needs to be present on a web page, which is an essential condition in using a web locator. Before automating any tests, you need to identify or trace out specific web elements among many others present in a web application or on a web page. Locators identify a specific web element.

A locator is a simple function or method by Selenium WebDriver. Locators identify web elements using different attributes supported by Selenium. There are eight unique locators (functions) to identify web elements, which are described next.

These functions provide the flexibility to trace or identify web elements to secure a script. Let's look at the different ways in which a web element can be located.

Locating Elements

A web page is built using elements like links, fields, text, images, and so forth. These elements are in the form of tags in HTML and sometimes not in HTML. To locate these elements, Selenium uses locators.

The eight types of locators that have been described in this chapter. The syntaxes, how, when, and where to use these locators are explained to enables you to utilize them in test cases later on.

Let's look at each of these web locators separately.

ID Locator

This method or function is one of the most widely used locators. IDs are unique attributes in an HTML web page and are less likely to be impacted by change. It is one of the easiest and most preferred means to locate an element on an HTML page.

According to W3C, every element must have a unique ID; however, browsers allow an exception to this rule. This exception allows different elements to have the same ID name or one with no ID, which is why Selenium has eight locators. The following is the syntax.

```
var_name = find_element_by_id ('id_attribute')
```

Consider the following HTML page source.

```
<html>
<body>
<form id="EmployeeForm">
<input name="employee_name"type="text"/>
<input name="email"type="email"/>
<input name="next"type="submit" value="Login"/>
</form>
</body>
</html>
```

In the HTML source code, the form tag is the only element that has an ID attribute. The form tag's ID attribute is named EmployeeForm. Using the syntax, the following code helps to trace/find an element with an ID attribute.

```
Employee_form = driver.find_element_by_id ('EmployeeForm')
```

By using this method, you can easily locate an element if the ID attribute is known. If multiple elements have the same ID attribute name, then the first matched ID is returned. If there is no match, then an exception is invoked. This exception is known as NoSuchElementException.

Name Locator

An element may have multiple attributes associated with it. The name attribute is a widely used attribute, but it may or may not be uniquely defined. The name attribute is usually an input element on a form (but also used in text fields and buttons). The name attribute passes all the corresponding values to the server when a submit action is performed on the form.

```
var_name = find_element_by_name ('name_attribute')
```

The following HTML source code shows how to locate an element with a name attribute.

```html
<html>
<body>
<form id="EmployeeForm">
<input name="employee_name" type="text" /><!--1st element-->
<input name="email" type="email" /><!--2nd element-->
<input name="next" type="submit" value="Login" /><!--3rd element-->
<input name="next" type="button" value="Clear" /><!--4th element-->
</form>
</body>
</html>
```

There are two input tags with name attributes. The first and second input tags (elements) have employee_name as a name attribute and email elements are easily located, as follows.

```python
#Locating first element
employee = driver.find_element_by_name('employee_name')

#Locating second element
email = driver.find_element_by_name('email')
```

In each case, the name locator is matched with the first element on the HTML source page. If no element on the page is matched, then NoSuchElementException is invoked.

In the case of multiple elements with the same name as an attribute, the locator chooses the first element on the HTML page bearing the exact specified name.

```python
next = driver.find_element_by_name('next')
```

From the earlier method, the Login button is returned because it appears before the Clear button. To return multiple elements from a page, please refer to the "Locating Elements" section.

XPath Locator

XPath is used in the XML language to locate nodes that navigate via elements and attributes. The paths are made of expressions associated with specific nodes. HTML also supports the implementation of XML using XHTML. In the absence of an ID and name, it is difficult to locate elements. In these situations, XPaths locators identify elements by their links. It is the third most-used locator after ID and name. There are a few ways to locate links because they are in a tree-like structure.

The general syntax for XPath is

```
xpath =//tag_name[@attribute_name= 'value']
```

- `//`: Defines the current directory/tag (a single slash is used for an absolute path)

- `tag_name`: Defines the name of the tag for the specified path

- `@`: Specifies the attribute to be selected

- `attribute_name`: Specifies the name of the attribute; the name of the attribute of the node

- **value**: Defines the value of the specified attribute

To better understand Xpath, you need to know the XML document. The XML document is tree-shaped structure with various attributes and tags associated with it. The following shows a tree-shaped structure of employees in the form of an XML document.

```
<employee>
<department = "Testing">
<fname>John </fname>
<lname>Wick</lname>
<title>Senior Tester</title>
<salary>$10000</salary>
</department>

<department = "Development">
<fname>Harry</fname>
<lname>Potter</lname>
```

```
<title>Junior Developer</title>
<salary>$5000</salary>
</department>
</employee>
```

The nodes form the tree-like structure. These nodes have a single root node from which the DOM structure begins. The other nodes are considered leaf or child nodes.

Note   The root node is also called the *parent node*, *start node*, or *initial node*.

The XML document structure is represented in Figure 4-1.

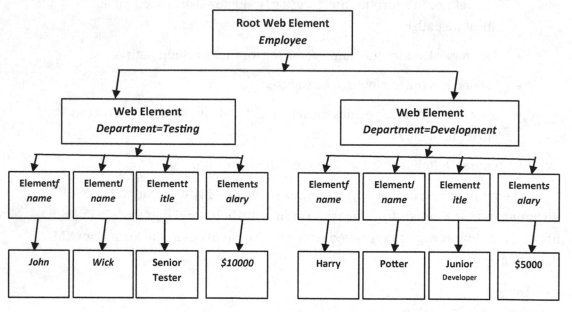

Figure 4-1. *Document Object Model of XML document structure*

The XML document contains only one root web element that is an *employee*. The employee web element has two nodes as departments: *testing* and *development*. These departments are also known as an attribute to the root element.

Each department contains four other attributes: fname, lname, title, and salary. These four attributes are associated with their respective values. The values for the employee in the testing department are as follows: fname is John, lname is Wick, title is Senior Tester, and salary is $10000. Similarly, for the development department, the values are Harry, Potter, Junior Developer, and $5000.

The following XML page source consists of various tags and attributes. You also need to know a little more terminology, as described in the next sections.

Nodes

In web pages, a tree-like structure represents the DOM. The nodes interconnect from the start to the end of the structure. The initial node is known as the *root node*. It is sometimes called an *initial node*.

In HTML, the `<html>` tag is the root node or initial node from where the node starts.

Parents

The web element embedded between the start and the end tags has a parent element associated with it. Any element except the root node has at least one parent. The head and body tags have an HTML tag as a parent, which is a root element.

Children

The parent element can have one or more children. The head, body, and div tags have children associated with them. Sometimes, a parent has no children, as in the case of a title tag.

Siblings

The web elements that belong to the same parent are known as *siblings*. For example, all the tags in a div tag are siblings.

Atomic Values

A web element with no parent or children is known as an *atomic value*. The best example is a root node with no children.

XPath Methods

The XPath axes help navigate or locate the web element by using the structural tree mechanism the same way as in XML. The dynamic nature of web elements makes it difficult to locate the XPath, and hence, the axes method solves this issue.

XPath axes have 13 different ways to locate complex or dynamic web elements.

Child

It locates all the child elements available that are associated with the current or selected web element on the web page/application.

Parent

It locates the parent element of the current web element. If the current element does not have any parent element, then the root node is considered its parent element. The root element is the parent to all the elements available.

Self-Axis

It only detects only one web element (i.e., itself).

Ancestor

It locates all the web elements starting from the parent of the current element to all its available ancestors (i.e., parent, grandparent, great-grandparent, etc.). It has a root element in it unless it is the root element.

Ancestor-or-Self

In this case, all available ancestors of the selected web element are located, including the current element.

Descendant

It locates all child web elements. The descendants include the children and grandchildren of the current element.

Descendant or Self

It includes the current element with all its children. If there are no children, then only the current element is returned.

Following

It locates all the web elements that come after the current element. It does not include the current element.

Following Sibling

It locates all the web elements at the same level after the current element. For example, any select box or radio button elements.

Preceding

It locates all web elements that occur before the current element on the page.

Preceding Sibling

It locates all the sibling elements that are present before the selected element of the same level.

Attribute

Once the web element has been located by using the attribute, this attribute is checked for the specified element. If it matches, then the element is returned; otherwise, it returns a null value.

Namespace

It locates all the web elements associated with the namespace. It is one of the least-used XPath axes.

Note   A web element with no child element (i.e., ( )) is called a *leaf node*.

Node Example

The following HTML defines a structure and its relationships. The relationship is illustrated in Figure 4-2.

```
<html><!-- Root node-->

<head><!-- Parent -->

<!--Child of head tag-->
<title></title>

</head>
```

```
<body><!-- Parent -->

<!--<div>Child of body
And Parent of header, section, aside, footer -->
<div>
                <!—Child one-->
<header>

</header>

<!—Child two-->
<section>

</section>

<!—Child three-->
<aside>

</aside>

                <!—Child four-->
<footer>

</footer>

<!-- The four tags header, section,
aside and footer are siblings to each other -->
</div>

</body>

</html><!-- End Node -->
```

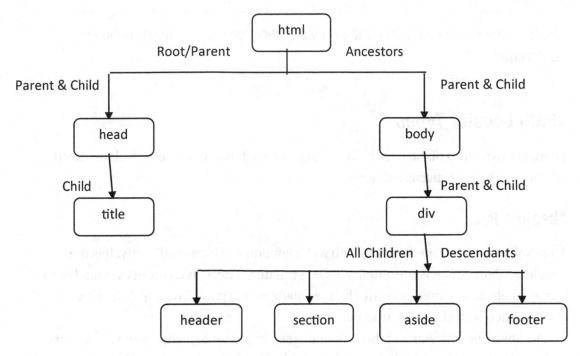

Figure 4-2. *Relationship among HTML tags*

The root or start node is the initial HTML tag. The HTML tag has two child elements: head and body. The head has only one child element title. The head is a child to the HTML tag and parent to the title, respectively. The head and body tags are siblings.

Similarly, the body has one child element: div. The div tag has four children. The div is a child of the body tag and parent to four child elements: header, section, aside, and footer. These four elements are siblings and do not have any of their own child elements. The div tag has no sibling.

The HTML is an ancestor to all the elements stated. Similarly, the head and body are ancestors to only their child elements. The title and div elements are grandchildren of the HTML element. The head has no grandchild. The body has four grandchildren. The child(ren) and grandchild(ren) are descendants of the parent and grandparent, respectively. Likewise, parent elements are the ancestors of child(ren) and grandchild(ren).

The header is a preceding sibling to the other three siblings. The footer is the following sibling to the first three siblings. Similarly, the head and body are preceding and following siblings, respectively.

Note   XPath is dependent on the browser because each browser behaves differently.

XPath Locator Types

There are two types of locators in XPath that are available to locate web elements in Selenium. They are discussed next.

Absolute Path

An *absolute path* is a method in which web elements are located directly. It is the simplest XPath, and it is present in a DOM structure. The web elements are unable to locate an element if there are any changes made in this path. The absolute path is the trail in which web elements are available.

An absolute path starts at the root node (i.e., initial node). The connection between nodes is indicated by a single forward-slash (/). The path is in a hierarchical order that begins with the top node.

Consider the following HTML code that shows how an absolute path is derived.

```html
<html>
<title></title>
<head></head>
<body>

<form id="EmployeeLogin">
<input name="fname" type="text" value="First Name"/><!--Input1-->
<input name="lname" type="text" value="Last Name"/><!--Input2-->
<input name="email" type="text" value="Email"/><!--Input3-->
<input type="text" name="location" value="Location"><!--Input4-->
<input name="password" type="password"/><!--Input5-->
<input name="continue" type="submit"
          value="Employee Login"/> <!--Input6-->
</form>

</body>
</html>
```

The absolute path locates the input of a location field in the HTML code. The input field is at the number 4 location, so its absolute path is

```
form_element= driver.find_element_by_xpath
                         ("/html/body/form/input[4]")
```

Note   In Selenium, indexing starts at one not zero.

In the preceding absolute path, the path starts at the root node (i.e., HTML node) and ends at the input[4] node, which is the web element to be located. Here the desired web element is the location field, which is at the end node of the described path.

Note   The absolute path starts at the root node and ends at the node that needs to be located.

Relative Path

In a relative path, web elements are located in the DOM structure, which makes it less susceptible to changes. A relative path can help locate web elements more easily than an absolute path.

XPath can start from anywhere within the web page (i.e., DOM structure) and ends at the node in which the web element needs to be located. The nodes are separated by a double slash (//) between them rather than a single slash.

Note   In a relative path, the current directory is taken as a reference.

A relative path uses a shorter path than an absolute path to locate web elements. To locate the location field, as stated in the preceding HTML code, the relative path for the same is as follows.

```
form_element= driver.find_element_by_xpath
                          ("//form//input[4]")
```

Here the node starts at the form element and ends at the fourth input field. The end is the element to be located.

Note   Slashes easily distinguish absolute and relative paths. In Xpath, a single slash means an absolute path, and a double slash means a relative path.

XPath with Logical Operators

XPath expressions with logical operators allow you to check or locate more than one web element on a web page. The logical operator is also known as a Boolean operator because it may or may not return the specified element. At least two XPath expressions are required for web elements to use logical operators, and therefore a logical operator can locate one or more web elements. The returning of web elements depends on the conditions specified.

The results of the specified conditions are true or false. When the result is true, then it returns a web element or else does not return any element. The two primary logical operators are described next.

AND

The AND logical operator returns or locates a web element when both XPath specified attributes match or are available (present) on the given web page; otherwise, it returns no web element. If either web element or its attributes are unavailable, then NoElementFoundException occurs. and is the keyword used for this operator.

```
form_element=driver.find_element_by_xpath("//input[@name='fname'
                                            and @type='text']")
```

In the example, the input web element is returned when it matches the name and type attributes associated with it. Table 4-1 shows when an element is located.

Table 4-1. *AND Conditions with Results for Web Elements*

A	B	Result
False	False	Locates No Element
True	False	Locates No Element
False	True	Locates No Element
True	True	Locates Both Elements (A&B)

Similarly, when the AND logical operator is used to return multiple web elements as a result by specifying two attributes related to them, it returns a False value. This can be verified and is achieved when the attributes belong to different elements. The following is another example showcasing XPath returning multiple web elements.

```
form_elements=driver.find_elements_by_xpath("//input[@name='fname'and
@name='lname']")
```

Two web elements are located by their name attributes.

OR

In this logical operator type, when either of the two specified attributes or web elements are available on a web page, it returns the web element for true Boolean values only. It returns no element when both conditions are false. The keyword is or. The following is a simple example in which the attributes for the input form is checked using the OR logical operator.

```
form_elements=driver.find_elements_by_xpath("//input[@name='fname'] or
                        [@name='newpassword']")
```

This example checks for two attributes—name and type, which are associated with input forms. If any of the attributes belong to any of the input forms stated, then it returns the respective web element. In this case, the input box number one (Input1) is returned, whereas there is no input form having a newpassword name attribute as its type.

Table 4-2 shows the logical values for web elements.

Table 4-2. *OR Conditions with Results for Web Elements*

A	B	Result
False	False	Locates No Element
True	False	Locates Element A
False	True	Locates Element B
True	True	Locates Both Elements (A&B)

Similarly, three different attributes of an input form have been mentioned with or logical operators. The attributes of web elements compared are name and type. All the attributes belong to each different web element from the given input form; hence it returns all associated input forms.

```
form_elements=driver.find_elements_by_xpath("//input[@name='fname'] or
                    [@name='lname'] or [@type='email']")
```

In the or logical code snippet, the first three input forms from one to three are retrieved as a result. The use of logical operators is not restricted in Selenium and hence can be used for multiple web elements.

Note   Both logical operators are case sensitive (i.e., and, or).

Types of XPath Functions

There are many web elements in a web application/page, which can make locating elements with the same attributes problematic; for example, several buttons with the same attributes, such as names or IDs. To locate these web elements, Selenium provides Xpath functions. Preferably, these functions are used with dynamically changing web elements. A few commonly used XPath functions are discussed next.

contains()

contains() is a method used for dynamically changing values in attributes associated with web elements in HTML pages. It is used when you know a partial attribute value or the partial link text that is implemented in the XPath. The contains() function searches for the given text on a web page and returns the web element if matched. It is generally used on the login page where the login ID changes dynamically.

The syntax for the `contains()` function is

```
//xpath[contains(@attribute, 'attribute value')]
```

The following is an example of `contains()` in complete and partial text.

```
//with complete text
element1 =driver.find_elements_by_xpath("//input[contains(@id, 'fname']")

//with Partial Link
element2 =driver.find_elements_by_xpath("//input[contains(@name, 'pass']")
```

Using our previous form HTML example, the web elements in this snippet searches for text and returns input1 for `element1` and input5 for `element2`. You need to understand that `element2` was provided with partial text ('pass'), which matches the name attribute of form input ('password'). Therefore, the partial text allows you to locate dynamic web elements.

text()

In the case of missing attributes in a web element, the `text()` function allows you to locate the elements by identifying certain text. The web element with this text is located.

```
//xpath[text() = 'login-in']
```

The following html code snippet uses the `text()` function to trace a web element.

```
<button type="button"> Submit <button/>
```

```
element3 =driver.find_elements_by_xpath("//button[text() = 'Submit']")
```

The button tag has no attributes; it only has text associated with it. The `text()` function is used to locate this element. `element3` retrieves the button with `'submit'` text related to it.

starts-with( )

This function is very similar to the contains function; the only difference is that it starts with checks for the initial string provided after XPath. This function is ideal for web elements whose values vary after a page reload. The initial string or text is matched to locate the web element.

The following is a general syntax example.

```
//xpath[starts-with(@attribute, 'attribute value')]
```

```
element4 =driver.find_elements_by_xpath("//form[starts-with(@id, 'Employee']")
```

The string of `id` for `element4` is the initial value and is matched with the available form ID on the page.

CSS Selectors

CSS selectors and XPath are similar because both can detect complex web elements on a web page. CSS selectors are easier to implement than XPath because CSS is not related to the DOM and has more flexibility with locating web elements. When a web page has a lot of CSS integrated into it, it is easy to use CSS selectors for locating web elements. It is robust too.

Note   CSS is the acronym for Cascading Style Sheets. It is a major component in making HTML pages attractive.

A CSS selector is formed by combining an element selector and its corresponding value. This corresponding value locates or identifies a web element within a page. The value may be in the form of an ID, a tag, an attribute value, and so forth.

When CSS selectors are used to locate a web element, the first element from the web page is returned when matched with the specified attribute. If no elements are corresponding to specified conditions, then an exception is raised. The general syntax for CSS selectors is

```
find_element_by_css_selector()
```

The following methods showcase some of the formats related to CSS selectors used to locate web elements.

ID

When a CSS selector is used with the ID attribute, a hash (#) symbol is placed between the HTML tag and the ID attribute. The symbol is used only for the ID attribute. The general syntax for CSS with an ID attribute is

```
<HTML_tag>#<ID_value>
```

Here is example HTML.

```
<pid="press">Apress Publication </p>
```

You can locate web elements using a CSS ID locator.

```
press=driver.find_element_by_css_selector('p#press')
```

There are a few different ways that it can be used in place of the preceding script, and the same can locate web elements too.

```
press=driver.find_element_by_css_selector("p[id = 'press']")
```

```
press=driver.find_element_by_css_selector("p#id='press'")
```

Class

A CSS selector can be used with a class attribute to locate a web element. A dot (.) is used the between the HTML tag and the class attribute. The syntax for CSS with class is

```
<HTML_tag>.<class_name>
```

In the following html code snippet, a CSS selector locates a paragraph element.

```
<html>
<body>

<p class="press ">Apress Publication </p>

//HTML tag with multiple CSS classes
<p class="my-class text-justify">New York</p>

</body>
</html>

press=driver.find_element_by_css_selector('p.press')
```

The 'press' variable locates the web element using a CSS locator. A dot symbol (.) combines multiple classes as one CSS selector. It also distinguishes attributes from values.

Similarly, you can locate a web element that has multiple CSS classes. The following are various ways to write this.

```
press1 =driver.find_element_by_css_selector('p.container')
```

```
press1 =driver.find_element_by_css_selector('p.my_class')
```

```
press1 =driver.find_element_by_css_selector('.my_class')
```

```
press1 =driver.find_element_by_css_selector('my_class.container')
```

```
press1 =driver.find_element_by_css_selector('container.p')
```

All the CSS locator scripts return the same web element.

Substring Match Cases

Web elements can have dynamic properties and tend to change for certain instances that occur from time to time. To locate these elements, default CSS is not an option because it uses static values for ID, class, and name.

The symbols that are accepted by CSS selectors are described in Table 4-3.

Table 4-3. *Substring Character with Description*

Symbol	Character Name	Description
^	halt	Matches the prefix of a string
$	dollar	Matches the suffix of a string
*	asterisk	Matches the string by using a substring
:	colon	Matches the string by using the contain() method

All the substring methods are applied in the following snippet of html script. These substrings match the IDs that are described in Table 4-3.

```
<p id="apress_press"></p>
<p id="apress_123"></p>
<p id="123_apress_press"></p>
```

The following shows a CSS selector locating with a substring.

```
#Using Halt '^' for suffix
press3 =driver.find_element_by_css_selector("p[id^='123']")
```

```
#Using Dollar '$' for prefix
press3 =driver.find_element_by_css_selector("p[id$='press']")
```

```
#Using Asterisk '*' for all
press3 =driver.find_element_by_css_selector("p[id* ='_apress_']")
```

```
#Using Colon ':' for contain method
press3 =driver.find_element_by_css_selector("p:contains('_apress_')")
```

These four substring methods are important when the complete string pattern is not known to tester.

Inner Text

The colon character with the `contains()` function can retrieve web elements by matching text present between HTML tags. This text is called *inner text*.

This method matches the plain text written between the start and end HTML tags. The element is located using the text that may be anywhere on a page, which is the same as the `contain()` function in the substring discussed.

```
<p>Apress</p>
```

```
press5 =driver.find_element_by_css_selector("p:contains('Apress')")
```

`contains` function is written with text that returns the web element containing it. The text may be complete or partial.

CSS Selector for Multiple Attributes

There are times when locating a web element with a single attribute is difficult as different web elements have same attribute value. This can be solved by using CSS Locator with multiple attributes associated to a particular web element.

Here is example HTML code.

```
<p class ="container" id="apress" style="align-self: center;"></p>
```

Here is the selector in action.

```
press4 =driver.find_element_by_css_selector("p[class= 'container']
[id='apress'][style='align-self:center']")
```

In this code snippet, multiple attributes and its associated values of tag are stated to locate it.

CSS Selector for Child Elements

Like the child elements that were discussed with XPath, CSS selectors can also locate child elements on a web page. To identify or locate a child element, the Selenium provides special symbols that are used with CSS selectors.

If a web element has one child element, then the greater-than symbol (>) is used, wherein XPath uses slashes.

```
<div class="cars">
<button id=Aston>
</div>
```

The preceding is an example of a web element with one child element. The HTML is div.cars>a, where div is the parent and button is its only child.

Here's the sample HTML.

```
<div id="cars">
<a href="#aston_martin">Aston</a>
</div>
```

XPath uses //div//a to locate a web element, while CSS selector uses a space instead of slashes.

```
cars = driver.find_element_by_css_selector("div#cars a")
```

When there are multiple child elements with no ID or names associated with them, elements are located through indexing, also known as the *nth element type*. It allows an indexed element to be located. The indexing starts at one.

```
<ol id="cars">
<li>Aston Martin</li>
<li>BMW</li>
<li>Chevy</li>
<li>Dodge</li>
</ol>
```

This ordered list has four child elements with no corresponding attributes. To locate these elements, indexing is done (starting at one). The elements to be located are the second, third, and fourth elements.

The following code shows the child elements to be located using a CSS selector.

```
#Locating second child element
car_no2 =driver.find_element_by_css_selector("ul#carsli:nth-of-type(2)")

#Locating third child element
car_no3 =driver.find_element_by_css_selector("ul#carsli:nth-of-type(3)")

#Locating last child element
last_cars=driver.find_element_by_css_selector("ul#carsli:last-child")
```

Assume that an element has *n* child elements, and you don't know the number of child elements associated with it. In this case, HTML attributes followed by the 'last-child' keyword is used to locate the last child of the parent element.

Link Locator

The link text locator is used to locate web elements that are available in an anchor tag (<a>). The anchor tag always defines a link that switches from one page to another, which is also known as a *hyperlink*. The href attribute in the anchor tag specifies the destination to which the page migrates to.

The link text locator tries to match the exact text available on the web page associated with the anchor tag. The syntax for link text locator is

```
find_element_by_link_text()
```

Note   Generally, the click() function accesses links in a web page/app.

The HTML code has anchor tags in it to which the link locator locates. The HTML is

```
<div class="container">Categories
        <a href="python.html">Python</a>
        <a href="web.html">Web Development</a>
        <a href="machine.html">Machine Learning</a>
        <a href="databases.html">Database</a>
</div>
```

The WebDriver link text locator locates the text *Python* or *Database,* which are associated with the destination addresses of python.html and database.html, respectively.

```
# Locate elements using link text
link1 =driver.find_element_by_link_text("Python")
link2 =driver.find_element_by_link_text("Database")
```

When there are multiple elements with the same text in anchor tags, the link locator retrieves the first matched element.

Note   Both link text and partial link locators are case sensitive.

Partial Link Locator

This partial link locator is very similar to a link locator. The only difference is that a partial link locator tries to match a substring from the text in an anchor tag on a web page. The syntax is

```
find_element_by_partial_link_text()
```

Note   Any link can be accessed by using either of the two link locators, regardless of whether the anchor tag is in or out of the block web elements.

The following is the partial text Python code for the same HTML anchor tags.

```
# Locate elements using partial link text
link3 =driver.find_element_by_partial_link_text("Pyt")
link4 =driver.find_element_by_patial_link_text("Data")
```

Pyt and *Data* are partial text for Selenium WebDriver to locate in elements within anchor tags. The partial text matches the text present on the web page; when matched, it returns the related element. Similarly, when the text is matched with more than one web element, the first element is returned as a result.

Note   When multiple web elements are present on a web page that has the same text defined in link text/partial link text locators, XPath or CSS selectors are used to locate the other web elements.

Tag Name

A web page/application is comprised of many HTML tags. These tags vary from element to element, but the use of the same tag on different web elements is permitted. In some cases, the tags enable you to locate the web element of choice. The syntax for a tag name is

```
find_element_by_tag_name()
```

The following is the tag name for associated HTML tags.

```
<html>
<head>
<title>Apress</title>
</head>
<body>
<h1>Python with Selenium</h1>
</body>
</html>
```

The Selenium tag name locator is

```
#Locating web element having <Title> tag
tag1 =driver.find_element_by_tag_name('Title')

#Locating web element having <h1> tag
tag2 =driver.find_element_by_tag_name('h1')
```

When there are multiple web elements with the same tags on a page, Selenium WebDriver locates the web element that first matches the specified tag. If there is no element named title or h1, then a no element exception is raised.

Class Name

The class name is used to locate web elements by stating the class name in the class function provided in Selenium. The class name is easily provided in the HTML tag. The class name locator is not a preferred way to locate web elements. The syntax is

```
find_element_by_class_name()
```

The following is a simple example of HTML with a Python class name locator.

```
<html>
<body>
<div class="my-class">Apress
<p class="text-justify">Python with Selenium</p>
</div>
</body>
<html>
```

The following is the Python code.

```
#For div element
class1 =driver.find_element_by_class_name('my_class')

#For paragraph Element
class2 =driver.find_element_by_class_name('text-justify')
```

Like other web locator behaviors for multiple elements, the class locator returns the first matched web element among many other elements in the same class. When no element is matched, an exception is raised. The syntax of all the locator's discussed has been given in Table 4-4.

Table 4-4. *Element Locators with Syntax*

Element Locator	Syntax
ID	find_element_by_id()
Name	find_element_by_name()
XPath	find_element_by_xpath()
Link	find_element_by_link_text()
Partial link	find_element_by_partial_link_text()
Tag name	find_element_by_tag_name()
Class name	find_element_by_class_name()
CSS selector	find_element_by_css_selector()

Note   When web locators are unable to locate web elements, NoSuchElementException is raised.

Locating Multiple Web Elements

When multiple web elements have the same name/ID/text/tag/class/link, then the first matched element is returned by Selenium WebDriver. To locate all the elements that are available on a page, Selenium provides a function/method for each locator. The syntax for each locator is listed in Table 4-5.

Table 4-5. *Syntax to Locate All Web Elements*

Element Locator	Syntax
ID	find_elements_by_id()
Name	find_elements_by_name()
XPath	find_elements_by_xpath()
Link	find_elements_by_link_text()
Partial link	find_elements_by_partial_link_text()
Tag name	find_elements_by_tag_name()
Class name	find_elements_by_class_name()
CSS selector	find_elements_by_css_selector()

The data type returned by the locators is a list. The following is an example that lists all the elements found using CSS selectors.

```
import requests
from selenium import webdriver

driver = webdriver.Firefox(executable_path=r'C:\Users\ADMIN\Desktop\
geckodriver.exe')

driver.get('https://apress.com')
images = driver.find_elements_by_css_selector("img")

for image in images:

        if (requests.head(image.get_attribute('src')).status_code == 200):
                print("Element Found.")
```

All the elements returned in a list are printed in a loop. The locator lists all the available web elements that are present on the Apress web page.

Locator Issues

There are instances when a web locator is unable to locate elements. The common issues of locators are discussed next.

Attribute Change

There are always changes in the behavior of a web element when certain actions are performed on it. These actions may be repetitive or new each time. Dynamic web elements develop a sophisticated experience. One example is that user events like mouse clicks or page reloads may result in different attribute values each time. These changes in the attribute value may prevent locating the web element needed. To locate these web elements, you must ensure that the locator returns the web element related to it despite any changes that occurred.

The default attribute are also changed by developers who implemented them in the internal framework of the web page/application. This enables to disintegrate the default XPath that is associated with that attribute on the page. To rectify such changes, you need to choose a different locator or check the path again.

No Web Element

In many cases, a web element is created when a certain event occurs, or actions have been achieved. A sign-out element is only available after the sign-out button is clicked. Similarly, the elements in a menu are available after a rollover or click action is performed by the user.

In these cases, the event triggers a web element's creation, so the action must be performed before using the locator.

Web Element Not Visible

Web elements are made available or visible after a page reload or actions are performed by the user, which is like no web element, but the web element exists on the page. When locators are applied and the locators are not visible, Selenium WebDriver returns a NoElementFound error.

To avoid these errors, the web elements are made visible by waiting, and then they can be located. Sometimes AJAX scripts are used to hide the elements, and these elements are located using waits. Waits are explained in Chapter 10.

Test Case Mismatch

There are certain times when a test case does not match with the locator conditions, or the test case executes faster than the web application and results in a No Web Element Found error. This is because the test case and the web app are not in sync to create or make a web element visible.

To solve the missing sync between the test case and web page/application, the test case halts until the required conditions are met, which makes the web element on the web page available.

iframe Web Element

When a web element is an iframe, or the iframe has an element in it, then locating these elements becomes difficult because frames are not easily accessible. When there are multiple frames available, identifying a specific frame is not easy. Even though they are available, the locator is unable to locate these frames and returns an error.

To locate iframes or elements in it, you need to identify all the available frames on the page and then switch to the frame to be located by using the `switchTo.frame()` function. After switching to the specified frame, you can locate the web element by using any of the locators.

Summary

Several kinds of web locators were discussed in this chapter. The ID and name locators are most often used because they are less prone to changes. The next important locator is XPath. You saw the structure of XPath in an XML document. A CSS locator was another important locator covered in this chapter.

The next chapter studies locating hyperlink web elements using the locators discussed in this chapter.

CHAPTER 5

Navigation

In the last chapter, we reviewed the various navigational links available on a web page that can be located using web locators. Some of the functionality and features were also discussed. This chapter explains web locator applications for finding navigational elements.

In web development, a hyperlink, or link, is a reference to data. This data is in the form of documents, videos, images, and so forth embedded in web elements. Navigation can be defined as an activity to migrate from one location to another. This migration can be within a web page or on another web page that has web elements in it. The process of navigation is done using hyperlinks.

A link is a URL (Uniform Resource Locator) displayed on a web page, whereas a hyperlink is created by placing a link in between anchor tags present in HTML. This chapter describes various ways in which a hyperlink is located and sets the criteria to test its presence on a web page embedded with different web elements.

The mechanisms in which a hyperlink is located are illustrated with a programming example. In the context of navigation used on a web page, you learn about hyperlinks and how they are defined on a web page.

Hyperlinks

Hyperlinks are primarily associated with menus, buttons, images, and documents to guide users to new locations/sections of the current web page or on another web page by using mouse action (like a click) or by submitting a form. In a few cases, a hyperlink is provided within a button to navigate when the form is completed.

There are various ways to use hyperlinks on a web page. Hyperlinks are incorporated in an HTML anchor tag that starts with <a> and ends with </a>. Any text can be written within the anchor tags. This text is displayed in a default blue color in browsers. Hyperlinks are also called *links*, which can be altered using CSS. The syntax is

```
<a href="URL">link text</a>
```

© Sujay Raghavendra 2021
S. Raghavendra, *Python Testing with Selenium*, https://doi.org/10.1007/978-1-4842-6249-8_5

Note   A hyperlink is also known as a *link*.

The following is an HTML example.

```
<div class="container">Selenium
<a href="python.html" id="python">Python</a>
<a href="elements.html" id="elements">Elements</a>
<a href="driver.html" id="driver">Driver</a><!-nth element>
</div>
```

Now that you know about hyperlinks, let's look at testing them using Python in Selenium.

Testing Hyperlinks

A Selenium test case checks whether a hyperlink is broken. A broken link is not reachable or does not function because of a server error. Hyperlinks are a connecting medium to different web pages and their associated elements.

Hyperlinks can be tested for the following points.

- Whether a link is available

- Whether a link navigates correctly to a specified page (a broken link) by getting a response from HTTP

- For document upload and form submissions that depend on hyperlinks

- Many links on a web page make manual testing time-consuming

---

Note   Linked text shows the presence of hyperlinks on a web page.

Web locators provide a stepping stone to locate hyperlinks. The various ways by which a hyperlink is located are discussed next.

Hyperlink by ID

A hyperlink can be located using an ID that is available in an anchor tag. When a web page is available in multiple languages, an ID is the best way to locate a hyperlink that has not changed. When a hyperlink is located, it needs to be clicked to navigate.

```
link1 =driver.find_element_by_id("python")
```

Hyperlink by Text

This syntax matches the complete string specified for the link. A string can be in any language apart from English, which sometimes returns an exception called NoSuchElementFound.

```
link2 =driver.find_element_by_link_text("Python")
```

Hyperlink by Partial Link

When a link needs to be located within a partial string, a partial link syntax is used. The string is matched with a substring present in the link.

```
# Locate elements using partial link text
link3 =driver.find_element_by_partial_link_text("Pyt")
```

Hyperlink by XPath

Links can be located using XPath (see Chapter 4), as follows.

```
link4 =driver.find_element_by_xpath("//a[@id= 'python']")
```

Nth Hyperlink

When there are multiple links available on a web page, you can choose the links using an index value. The links should be under the same tag and in sequential order when the index needs to be used. Links are under tags that cannot be identified or traced using an index value because tags change.

```
link5 = driver.find_element_by_xpath("//div/a[3]")
```

The index value changes when the positions of a link are altered, and hence, this method is less commonly used.

Note   Adding or removing links also alters the present index value.

Until now, we have located only individual hyperlinks using various web locators. If there is more than one hyperlink on a web page, then the methods return only the first matched hyperlink among them. To locate all the web elements, refer to Table 4-5 in Chapter 4.

Return All Hyperlinks

When there is more than one link available on a web page, a CSS selector is used to return all the links.

```
links=driver.find_elements_by_css_selector("a")
```

The hyperlinks need to be located by different locators before any check or validation is done to them. To check the presence of a hyperlink on a web page, you test the link using validation expressions, which are discussed next.

Check for a Valid Hyperlink

Verifying that a hyperlink is valid is done by using HTTP status code values. HTTP sends back a message corresponding to the values (see Table 5-1). When a link is broken, HTTP returns a 404 error (a Link or Page Not Found error).

```
import requests
from selenium import webdriver

driver=webdriver.Firefox()
driver.get("http://apress.com/")
links=driver.find_elements_by_css_selector("a")

for link in links:
```

```
if (requests.head(link.get_attribute('href')).status_code==200):
        print("Link is Valid")
else:
        print("Link is Invalid/Broken")
```

Similarly, you can check for images by changing the CSS selector value to img. HTTP status codes and their error descriptions are listed in Table 5-1.

Table 5-1. *HTTP Status Codes*

HTTP Code	Description
200	Valid Link
400	Bad Request
401	Unauthorized
404	Link/Page not Found
500	Internal Error

Check for Broken Images

A link can also be associated with images. A hyperlinked image can also be checked to see if it is broken or not by comparing with HTTP status code as it is done in case of only links.

```
import requests
from selenium import webdriver

driver =webdriver.Firefox()
driver.get("http://apress.com/")
images=driver.find_elements_by_css_selector("img")

for image in images:

        if (requests.head(imageget_attribute('src')).status_code==200):
                print("Valid Image Link.")
        else:
                print("Invalid Image Link.")
```

Hyperlinks can be validated using the status codes available in HTTP protocols (see Table 5-1). Now that you know about validating the presence of hyperlinks based on these protocols, let's check the respective data attributes associated with a hyperlink.

Data Attributes Hyperlink

The data attribute returns a link's text value. When the hyperlink element is not known, this command can get the data attribute value related to the hyperlink element.

The following is an HTML example.

```
<div class="hyper_links"><a href="python.html">Python</a></div>
```

The following is a Python example.

```
link1 =driver.find_element_by_css_selector("div.hyper_links a")
print (link1.text)
```

This test case returns the data attribute in Python, which is an attribute text value present between the anchor tags.

Note   Forms or document uploads have dynamic hyperlinks related to them.

Summary

This chapter defined hyperlinks, which are crucial for migrating to another section on a web page or to a new web page. The chapter also looked at the primary aspects of testing hyperlinks and the different ways by which hyperlinks can be located. You learned about locating multiple hyperlinks on a web page. Numerous validations can be performed on hyperlinks. The validations are based on HTTP status codes.

It is time to explore more distinct web elements that can be located and validated, like hyperlinks. The validations are a bit unique due to the method of selection. You learn about buttons in the next chapter.

CHAPTER 6

Buttons

Hyperlink locators used to jump to different sections or pages of a web application were discussed in the previous chapter. The same web locators are used to trace user interface elements like buttons. There are various buttons in a web application, which are described in this chapter.

Buttons are part of the user interface in any web application that interacts with a user/client. These interactions are associated with certain actions, such as moving to the next page and submitting forms. They include default buttons, form/submit button, radio buttons, checkboxes, and select lists. The differences among them depend on the usage, which is explained next.

The types of HTML buttons are located using Python on Selenium because web elements like these buttons have specific functionalities related to them. Let's start by learning about a default button on a web page.

Default Button

A default button is the most basic type available on an HTML web page. A default button is created using the `<button>` tag. The following code snippet allows you to create a default button. Figure 6-1 shows the output.

```
<button id="default_btn" class="default" name="dft_btn" style="font-size:21px;">Default Button</button>
```

Default Button

Figure 6-1. *Default button*

© Sujay Raghavendra 2021
S. Raghavendra, *Python Testing with Selenium*, https://doi.org/10.1007/978-1-4842-6249-8_6

A default button can have various functions, such as edit, delete, create, reset, and clear. Selenium performs two major operations on buttons.

- Select (locate elements and click)

- Assert (check for the button and whether enabled/disabled)

Select

Selecting and clicking a button is a way to locate the button element on a web page. A button is activated when clicked, and then it performs the assigned task to it.

Note   The button is always selected by using the click() method after locating it on the web page.

There is another method to click a button, which is discussed later in this chapter. A default button can be selected in any of the following ways.

Select by ID

As discussed in earlier chapters, an ID is a unique attribute, and it is used to easily locate a button element.

```
#Method 1
#Finding or Identifying Default Button
default_button=driver.find_element_by_id('default_btn')

#Clicking on the button selected
default_button.click()

#Method 2
#Identifying & Clicking Default Button
default_button=driver.find_element_by_id('default_btn').click()
```

The HTML code for the default button in Figure 6-1 is a source to locate the button element. There are two methods for it. In the first method, two functions are used, one for identifying the default button by using an ID, which is then selected by using the click() function (for more information, see Chapter 3).

In the second method, the same functions from the first method are combined in a single line of code. It is utilized in the rest of this chapter. The first method is more readable, whereas the second method is short. It is up to the tester to decide which one to use.

Note   These two methods have the same functionality and purpose.

The ID is stated when the developer is writing the code, which makes it simpler for the tester to use in testing cases.

By Text

This is the most basic selection mechanism for buttons. In this selection type, the default button is selected by using the text written to it, which is seen in the browser.

Figure 6-1 shows the button's text and its corresponding HTML code. The text always appears on the button when compiled in a browser. In HTML code, the text is placed between the start and end button tags. The following Python Selenium code selects a button by text.

```
#Using text ()
button_text=driver.find_elements_by_xpath
                    ("//button[text()='Default Button']").click()
```

The text on a button is also identified using the contain function with the text function.

```
#Using contain () with text ()
button_text1 =driver.find_elements_by_xpath("//
button[contains(text()='Default Button')]").click()
```

By Name

A button is selected by using the name attribute in HTML when an ID is not available. It is like locating web elements by name, as follows.

```
default_button=driver.find_element_by_name('dft_btn') .click()
```

When there are multiple buttons with same name, the first button bearing the name is selected.

Next, let's look at another type of button.

Submit/Form Button

A submit button submits the data inserted into a form. It is available at the end of the form. The form button is generally created by using the `<input>` tag or by having `submit` as a type in the button or input tags. When this button is clicked, it navigates to another page, or a popup message is displayed when used dynamically. Figure 6-2 shows a submit button with its corresponding source code.

```
<h1> Employee Form</h1>

<form>
  Employee Name:
<input type="text" id="ename" name="ename"><br><br>
  Employee Dept:
<input type="text" id="dept" name="dept"><br><br>
<input type="submit" value="Submit Button">
</form>
```

Employee Form

Employee Name: [   ]

Employee Dept: [   ]

[Submit Button]

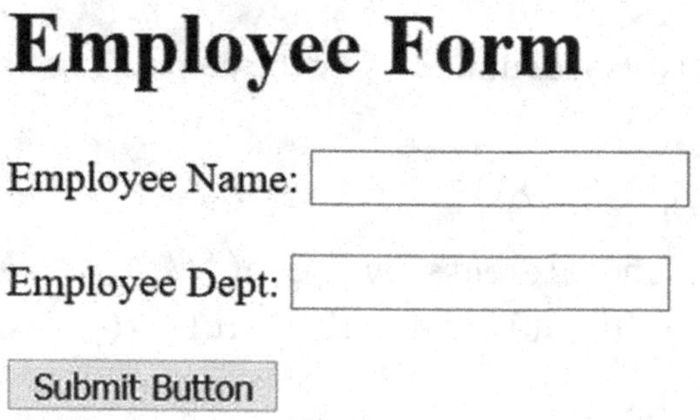

Figure 6-2. *Submit button*

The submit button does not work until all fields are filled, which makes it different from the default button.

Note   The click( ) function for a form button is successful only when all the form elements are filled.

Select by Visible Text

Selecting a submit button is like selecting a default button. Locating these elements is done following the same techniques. The following is a simple example of selecting a submit button by text.

```
submit_text=driver.find_element_by_xpath
                         ("//input[@value'Submit Button']").click()
```

XPath is used to locate the submit button by its text, which is case sensitive.

Image as a Button

A button can be created using an image. The image offers a customized look and feel to the user.

To use an image as a button, the input type must be an `image` with a `src` attribute defining the path of that image. It is used for both button types. The following is a simple example of a button created using an image.

```
<form>
<input type="image" id="img" name="img_btn"
                         src="images/go.jpg" alt="Go">
</form>
```

Figure 6-3 shows an image is used as a button. To select an image button, you use the following Python code in Selenium.

Figure 6-3. *Image as a button*

#Image Button
```
image_button=driver.find_element_by_xpath("//input[contains
                              (@src='images/go.jpg')]")
```

Note   Images can act as both submit or default types.

Assert for Button

The two main assert approaches for buttons are to verify the presence of a button element on a web page and to check if the element is disabled or not.

The assertion method determines whether the button is present on the given web page. A button can be present on a web page but also be disabled, which makes the button unable to be clicked. The click() function cannot operate on disabled buttons.

Check the Presence of a Button

The presence of a button lets you know whether a button element is available on the specified web page. It is essential to verify whether the specified attribute or path is still available for the button.

```
#Check if button is enabled or not
if default_button.is_displayed():
        print("Element is Present")
else:
        print("Element Not Present")
```

Check If the Button Is Enabled or Not

The form button is enabled after a form is completed when dynamically used with JavaScript. There are only rare instances in which a form button is disabled; it may be because the date to submit the form has expired, or only a limited number of forms can be submitted.

```
#Check if button is enabled or not
if default_button.is_enabled():
        print("Element is Enabled")
```

```
else:
        print("Element Not Enabled")
```

Checking its presence and whether a button is enabled or disabled is done using the `if-else` condition in Python on Selenium. These validations are the same for all button types.

Next, let's discussed the radio button, which is one of the most used buttons on a web page that offers choices.

Radio Buttons

Radio buttons are used when multiple choices are available. Each radio button has the same name attribute. When a radio button is selected from a collection, the others are automatically deselected. There is no limit on the number of radio buttons in a group or the number of groups that use radio buttons.

The following is the HTML source code of the radio button shown in Figure 6-4.

```
<h3>Select your Gender:</h3>

<div>
<input type="radio" id="male" name="gender" value="male"
checked>
<label for="male">Male</label>
</div>

<div>
<input type="radio" id="female" name="gender" value="female">
<label for="female">Female</label>
</div>

<div>
<input type="radio" id="other" name="gender" value="other">
<label for="other">Prefer not to Say</label>
</div>
```

Figure 6-4 shows that when a radio button is selected, a black dot appears in it. There is no dot in the unselected radio buttons. This helps you identify if the radio button was selected/checked or not. *Male* is checked by default as seen in the HTML source code. Selection is not mandatory in radio buttons.

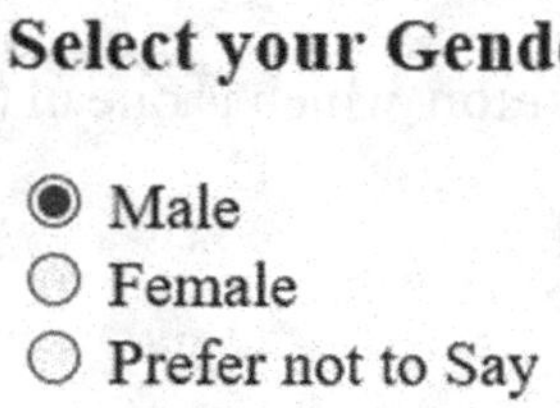

Select your Gender:

- ⦿ Male
- ○ Female
- ○ Prefer not to Say

Figure 6-4. *Radio buttons checked and unchecked*

Note   Selection and checked are referred interchangeably.

The attribute value presents the radio button's unique value, which is only showcased in the HTML code. The user cannot see it in a browser. The value is transmitted to the server.

Radio buttons have two main operations: to select and to deselect the selected. These two operations are demonstrated next.

Select Radio Buttons

There are various ways to select radio buttons that need to be tested among a group, which are explained as follows.

Simple Select

To select a radio button, you must locate the element and then click it. In this method, the radio button is selected using the ID attribute.

```
#Selecting female radio button
radio_button=driver.find_element_by_id("female")
radio_button.click()
```

The ID attribute selected is *female,* which is associated with the radio button provided in the HTML source. When clicked, a black dot appears in the selected radio button. A dot can be customized into various shapes and colors. The primary motive is to see that the radio button was selected.

Select Using Label

The label is an HTML tag that writes the plain text associated with a form web element. The plain text is written between the start and end tags of the label. This text can also be used to select the radio button.

```
#Using label attribute with for
radio_button=driver.find_element_by_xpath("//label[@for='female']").click()
```

The label tag is selected by using XPath and the value of the attribute related to it. The click function is used after locating the radio element.

Note   A black dot in a radio button shows that the button has been selected.

Unselect/Clear Selection

The radio button has two operations associated with it: one is to select, and the other is to deselect. A black dot is available only when a radio button is selected. To clear the selected radio button, you need to select another button because multiple selections are not allowed in the same collection of radio buttons.

The selection of another radio button from the group is made the same way as previous selection types. To avoid the unnecessary selection of radio buttons, a default selection is introduced in some cases.

Note   The only way to deselect an already selected radio button is to select another radio button from the group/collection.

83

Assert for Radio Button

If there is a group of radio buttons on a web page, to identify if one is checked or to make sure the specified radio element is available on the web page, assertions are used. Assertions play an important role in testing radio buttons and the actions corresponding to them.

Assert If a Radio Button

There are various ways to determine if a web element on a web page is a radio button. A common way is to use the attribute value of the input attribute. If the input type is radio, then the web element is a radio button.

```
#Locate Web element
radio_button=driver.find_element_by_id("female")

#If stmt to check attribute value
if radio_button.get_attribute("type") =="radio":
            print("It is a Radio button")
else:
            print("It is not a Radio button")
```

In this example, the web element with *female* as the ID is checked for its input type using the if statement from the get_attribute( ) function.

Assert If Checked

There are two ways where to assert if a radio button is selected or not. In the first method, the select function is used; it returns a true as the Boolean value if selected and false if not selected. The second method checks the radio button's attribute value, which is checked in the HTML source. When checked, it returns true; when not checked, it returns false.

```
#Using Selection function
driver.find_element_by_id("female").is_selected()

#Check using attribute function
driver.find_element_by_id("female").get_attribute("checked")
```

In some cases, a radio button has a default selection. In Figure 6-3, the default radio button is the first radio element, with male as the text. It can be checked by using the `if` statement, which returns Boolean values.

```
radio_button=driver.find_element_by_id("female")
if radio_button.get_attribute("checked") =="true":
                print('Radio Button is "Selected')
else:
                print('Checkbox is Not Selected')
```

The assertion method checks if the radio button is selected or not. But locating of buttons does not get affected by the type of button to be located using web locators.

Next, let's examine checkboxes.

Checkbox

Checkboxes have a square box associated with them. They are commonly used when multiple selections are required from the user. There are no restrictions on selecting checkboxes. You could select all the checkboxes in the same group/collection. The selection can also be restricted when necessary, however.

To make a checkbox in HTML, the input type is `checkbox`. This attribute type lets you know the presence of a checkbox during assertion.

```
<form>
<input type="checkbox" id="firefox" name="browser1" value=" b1" checked>
<label for="brower1"> Firefox</label><br>
<input type="checkbox" id="chrome" name="browser2" value="b2">
<label for="browser2"> Chrome</label><br>
<input type="checkbox" id="opera" name="browser3" value="b3">
<label for="browser3"> Opera</label><br>
<input type="checkbox" id="edge" name="browser4" value="b4">
<label for="browser4"> Edge</label><br><br>
</form>
```

Figure 6-5 shows checked and unchecked checkboxes. You know that the checkbox is selected when a tick symbol appears in the square box.

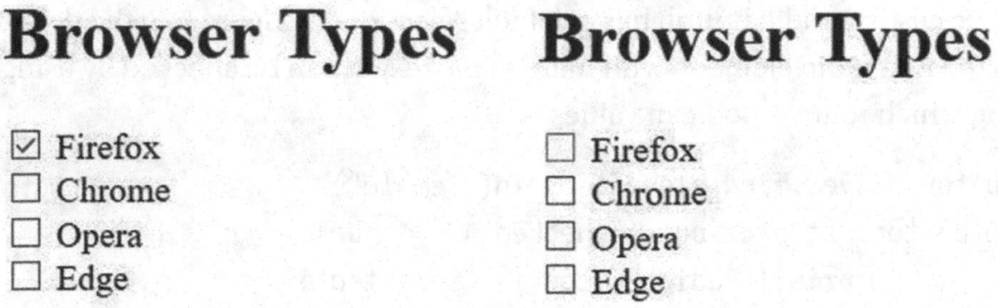

Browser Types   Browser Types

☑ Firefox   ☐ Firefox
☐ Chrome   ☐ Chrome
☐ Opera   ☐ Opera
☐ Edge   ☐ Edge

Figure 6-5. *Checkbox checked and unchecked*

Select/Check

Selecting a checkbox is like selecting a radio button. The difference is that multiple selections are allowed with checkboxes, but radio button selection is limited to one. A checkbox has various attributes associated with it. It is selected by clicking it.

Note   Checkboxes can have multiple selections related to the same group.

Check Using Name

A checkbox can be selected using the name attribute in the HTML source, as follows.

```
#Select Opera check button
check_button=driver.find_element_by_name("browser3").click()
```

Check Using ID

In this method, the ID attribute locates the checkbox element and then uses the click function to select it.

```
#Select Edge check button
check_button=driver.find_element_by_id("edge")
check_button.click()
```

Note   A tick mark appears when a checkbox has been selected.

Assert If Checkbox

The checkbox attribute type identifies an element as a checkbox, as shown in the following.

```
#Identify for Checkbox
check_button=driver.find_element_by_id("chrome")

if check_button.get_attribute("type") =="checkbox":
                print("It is a Checkbox button")
else:
                print("It is not a Checkbox button")
```

The get attribute function is used in if statement to check for the presence of a checkbox element.

Assert Checkbox If Checked or Not

The ways in which a radio button is checked also apply to a checkbox. The Python Selenium code for checkbox identification on a web page is as follows.

```
#Using Selection function
driver.find_element_by_id("firefox").is_selected()

#Check using attribute function
driver.find_element_by_id("firefox").get_attribute("checked")
```

Clear/Unselect/Deselect Checkbox

To remove the tick from a selected checkbox is to *deselect, unselect,* or *clear* it. These three terms are used interchangeably. Clearing the textbox is allowed in Python on Selenium, and it is used to test that the checkbox is working correctly. In some cases, the checkbox is disabled or is set to default, which does not allow you to clear it.

A checkbox must be selected before clearing it. This is done by using the same `click()` function again. To determine if a checkbox is selected or not, you can use the assert function.

```
#Clearing checkbox
check_button=driver.find_element_by_id('firefox')

#if condition to check selection
if check_button.is_selected():

        #Clear using click()
        check_button.click()
        print('Checkbox clicked to deselected')
else:

        print('Checkbox is not selected')
```

In this code, the checkbox is recognized if it has already been selected using the `if` condition statement; if selected, then it is cleared or unselected.

Note   Clearing the checkbox can be done only when it is selected.

All the methods used in checkboxes are the same ones available for radio buttons, apart from the clearing method. A radio button automatically clears after selecting another option. This is not the case with a checkbox; hence, clear/deselect is done by performing the same action used to select.

Next, let's discuss the select list.

Select List

The final button type is the select list. This button type can act as both a radio button or a checkbox when the user can select a single choice or multiple choice. A select list creates multiple options listed in a drop-down list. One or multiple options can be selected from the list. A select list is formed by combining the `<select>` and `<option>` tags, respectively. It is similar to a drop-down menu.

```
<h1>Blood Group</h1>
<label for="blood">Choose Blood Group:</label>

<select name = "blood" id = "bld_grp">
<option value = "A"> A type </ option>
<option value = "B"> B type </ option>
<option value = "O"> O type </ option>
<option value = "AB"> AB type </ option>
<option value = "Bombay"> Bombay type </ option>
</select>
```

Select lists are commonly used inside a form tag but can be used independently. The number of options that can be selected from the lists can be controlled. When only one option can be selected from a list, it behaves as a radio button. When multiple options can be selected from a list, it acts as a checkbox.

Figures 6-6 and 6-7 show a drop-down menu that lists five human blood types. The drop-down menu is opened by clicking it, which allows you to choose from it as well.

Blood Group

Choose Blood Group: | A type   ⌄ |

Figure 6-6. *Single select list*

Blood Group

Choose Blood Group: | A type   ⌄ |
                    | A type |
                    | B type |
                    | O type |
                    | AB type |
                    | Bombay type |

Figure 6-7. *Open select list*

Getting All the Options

You need to know all the options available in a list. This is done by using the following code.

```
s = driver.find_elements_by_tag_name("option")

for option in s:
    print("Option is: %s" % option.get_attribute("value"))
```

As stated in the code, the for loop returns all the options in the blood group select list.

Select

Python in Selenium provides many ways to select from the available options. Before selecting the select list from the web page/app, you need to import the *select* library from selenium.webdriver.support.select in Python. The selection methods are discussed next.

Select Using Visible Text

The text that is visible in a drop-down list can be used as a medium to select the options.

```
#Importing Select Library
from selenium.webdriver.support.select import Select

# First Select ID of drop-down
select_list=Select(driver.find_element_by_id('bld_grp'))

# select by visible text
select_list.select_by_visible_text('O type')
```

In the selection process of a drop-down/select list, the drop-down menu is located first. Then, an instance is created to select an option from the list. The drop-down can be located using several attributes, such as ID and name.

Select by Value

The value attribute associated with each option is different. These attribute values select the option. The available values in the select list are A, B, O, AB, and Bombay.

```
# Select drop-down ID
select_list=Select(driver.find_element_by_name('blood'))

# Select by visible text
select_list.select_by_value('O')
```

The value attributes are case sensitive and allow alphanumeric characters.

The O blood type needs to be selected. This is done by first selecting the drop-down in which the option is located, and then the instance is created to select the specified option.

Select Using Index

The options in the select list have index values that are not specified in the HTML code. Selenium allows you to select an option using these index values. The index value starts at 0 and is related to the first option in the select list.

```
# Selecting Drop-down
select_list=Select(driver.find_element_by_id('bld_grp'))

# Selecting last option Bombay by index value
select_list.select_by_index('4')
```

An index value of 4 selects the last option in the drop-down list. To select options using an index value, you need to know the number of available options in the drop-down.

To select the last option in the drop-down list, use a –1 index value, which is commonly used in Python.

```
# Selecting last option Bombay by index value
select_list.select_by_index('-1')
```

Note   The select method in Python on Selenium cannot be used if the list was not built using the select tag.

Unselect/Clear/Deselect

The options selected from a list can revert by clearing it. Unselecting/deselecting/ clearing (the terms are synonymous) an option in a select list can be done the same way the selection was made. The list may allow single or multiple selections.

Deselect/Clear One Selected

Deselection can be made to single or multiple options in the list. The following discusses deselecting/clearing a single option.

Deselect by Visible Text

The text that is visible in a list can be accepted as a value to deselect it when selected.

```
#clear using index
clear= Select(driver.find_element_by_id('bld_grp'))

clear.deselect_by_index('Bombay')
```

The last option, Bombay, is deselected using a visible text function.

Deselect by Value

When a specified value matches the value attribute in the list, that list element is deselected.

```
#clear by value
clear= Select(driver.find_element_by_id('bld_grp'))

clear.deselect_by_value ('0')
```

There are two possible exceptions may be raised in this case, one when there is no match for the defined value. The second exception is raised after the value is matched but the list element is not selected as deselect works only if list is selected.

Deselect by Index

An option in a list is deselected using its index value. Similar to selecting an option with the index value, an option can also be cleared/deselected.

```
#clear by index
clear= Select(driver.find_element_by_id('bld_grp'))

clear.deselect_by_index('4')
```

The last element in the list is cleared if selected; otherwise, an exception is raised.

Multiple Select List

A select list may allow multiple options to be selected. The HTML source and its corresponding output are shown in Figure 6-8. In multiple selections, there are seven options available and among them four have been selected. The code for selecting these options are made as follows. all_options cannot be used as it selects all available list.

```html
<h1>Fruit Salad</h1>

<label for="fruits">Choose Multiple Fruits:</label>
<select id="fruits" name="fruits" size="7" multiple>
<option value="apple">Apple</option>
<option value="banana">Banana</option>
<option value="cranberry">Cranberry</option>
<option value="dragonfruit">Dragon Fruit</option>
<option value="elderberry">Elderberry</option>
<option value="figs">Figs Fruit</option>
<option value="grapes"> Grapes</option>
</select>
<br><br>

<p>For Windows, hold the Ctrl button while selecting options. For Mac, hold
the Command button while selecting options.</p>
```

Fruit Salad

Choose Multiple Fruits:

For Windows, hold the Ctrl button while selecting options.

For Mac, hold the Command button while selecting options.

Figure 6-8. *Multiple select list*

In multiple selections, there are seven options available, and out of them, four have been selected. The selections are made as follows in the code.

```
ticks = Select(driver.find_element_by_id('fruits'))

#Selecting Options in different ways
ticks.select_by_index(0)

ticks.select_by_value ('cranberry')

ticks.select_by_visible_text('Elderberry')

ticks.select_by_index(6)
```

Verify

Assertion functions are used to avoid exceptions that arise in an element not found, or when the element needs to be deselected when not selected and vice versa. These kinds of exceptions can be avoided using option functions that let you know the type of list and whether it is selected or not.

Get the First Option Selected

The first option that is selected in a multiple select list or the current selected option in a single select list is returned.

```
selected_list=Select(driver.find_element_by_id('bld_grp'))
```

```
#Prints first selected option value
print (selected_list.first_selected_option.get_attribute('value'))
```

The print statement prints the first selected option from the list and returns an error if no option is selected.

Get All Options Selected

To get all selected options from the list, a function named `all_selected_options()` is used.

```
selected_list=Select(driver.find_element_by_id('bld_grp'))
```

```
#Returns all selected options
selected_list.all_selected_options()
```

It is mainly used in a multiple select list that returns all selected options.

Deselect/Clear All Selected

This function clears/deselects all the selected options from the drop-down list. It is mainly used with multiple selections in a list. When no multiple selections are available, a NotImplementError exception is raised.

```
#Clear all selected
clear= Select(driver.find_element_by_id('bld_grp'))
```

```
clear.deselect_all()
```

To clear all the selected options in a list, Selenium provides the `deselect_all()` function.

Note   The select method in Python on Selenium cannot be used if the list is not built using the select tag.

Summary

This chapter explains the mouse/keyboard actions and web locators discussed in Chapters 3 and 4 that are most often used on a user interface (i.e., the buttons in a web application). The web locators find all types of buttons available, and corresponding actions are performed on them.

The default button, when located, is only allowed to perform click action. The Submit button is used for forms. The radio button provides multiple choices but allows only one selection among them. Checkboxes allow multiple choices and selections. A select list is a button further classified into two types based on the single or multiple selections in it. Each button was illustrated with an example.

Locating UI web elements like frames and textboxes are discussed in the next chapter.

CHAPTER 7

Frames and Textboxes

The previous chapter explained how to locate buttons like default, radio, checkbox, and select list. Each button has a functionality associated with it, such as submit, select, or deselect. Button functionalities are performed with a click action from a mouse (see Chapter 3). This chapter discusses locating web elements like frames and textboxes. It also explains handling single and multiple frames on a web page.

The chapter also covers textbox types, relevant Selenium WebDriver commands, and value insertion.

Iframe

An iframe is another web element available in HTML. It is widely used for embedding media-related web elements (videos, images, etc.) on a web page. YouTube videos and advertisements are two of the most popular examples of embedded videos and images the web pages.

A frame can embed any HTML web element. Frames can be nested within one another. Iframes are defined using the `<iframe>` tag at the start and the `</iframe>` tag at end.

Note Iframes are important to test because they often have web elements that are embedded from other web sites or sources.

To test with web elements that are present in an iframe, you need to switch to that particular frame. It is difficult to locate an iframe because it is in a DOM-like structure. When there are multiple iframe elements in a stack structure, switching to the related iframe gives access to the web elements present within it.

Note An *inline frame* is another term used to describe an iframe.

© Sujay Raghavendra 2021
S. Raghavendra, *Python Testing with Selenium*, https://doi.org/10.1007/978-1-4842-6249-8_7

In previous versions of HTML, frameset tags contained the frame tags, but an iframe does not require these tags. One major difference is that iframes can have nested iframes in it, which was not allowed in frames. In Selenium, frames and iframes are treated the same; hence, only iframes are tested in this chapter.

A simple example of an iframe in HTML is shown in Figure 7-1.

```
<iframe id="new_frame" name="apress" src="https://www.apress.com"
height="300" width="300"></iframe>
```

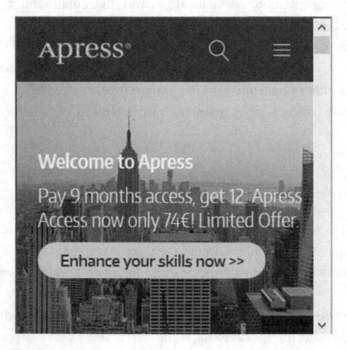

Figure 7-1. *A single iframe*

The preceding code displays the Apress web site in an iframe. You can see that the iframe contains the link to the site. The source (`src`) attribute may have web elements that are within or outside of the web page. The height and width can be in pixels or percentages; here, the pixels are used.

Note   Frame and frameset tags were deprecated in HTML5. Iframes are used instead.

Switching to Iframe

Similar to locating web elements, iframes can be located using the switch function. When a defined iframe is switched, then only tests can be performed on any web element present inside that iframe. Many web pages use iframes because there is no need to reload or refresh the page after interacting with an iframe. The following sections describe ways to switch to an iframe in Python with Selenium.

Switching Using ID

An iframe can be located using the ID attribute, which is done using a switch function. Python in Selenium is applied to the previous code. The value for the ID attribute is new_frame.

```
# Switch to the frame with id attribute
driver.switch_to_frame("new_frame")
```

Switching Using Name

The name attribute can also be used to locate an iframe on a web page.

```
# Switch to frame with name attribute
driver.switch_to_frame("apress")
```

Switching Using Index

If a web page contains more than one iframe (see Figure 7-2), switching to a defined iframe is done using an index value. This index value is provided by Selenium. The following is the HTML code for multiple frames.

```
<center>
<div><h5>Frame0</h5>
<iframe id="new_frame0" name="apress" src="https://www.apress.com"
height="150" width="400"></iframe>
</div>
<div><h5>Frame1</h5>
```

```
<iframe id="new_frame1" name="bing" src="https://www.bing.com" height="150"
width="400"></iframe>
</div>
<div><h5>Frame2</h5>
<iframe id="new_frame2" name="wiki" src="https://www.wikipedia.org"
height="150" width="400"></iframe>
</div>
```

Frame0

Frame1

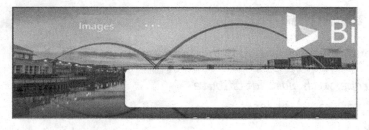

Frame2

Figure 7-2. *Multiple iframes*

Here is the Python code.

```
# Switch to frame 1
driver.switch_to_frame(0)
```

```
# Switch to frame 2
driver.switch_to_frame(1)
```

```
# Switch to frame 3
driver.switch_to_frame(2)
```

This method is not recommended because there may be changes to a frame's position when other frames are added or removed from the web page.

Note   Selenium initializes the index value of an iframe on a web page from 0 (zero).

Switching as an Element

When multiple iframes on a web page have the same IDs and names, switching to a specific frame is difficult. In these cases, iframes can be identified by web elements. Web elements like ID and name are for switching to defined iframes.

Web element locators like XPath, CSS selectors, or classname are used to locate iframes. Other web locators, such as linkText or partialLinkText, cannot be used to locate iframes. A tag name web locator is not preferable when there are multiple iframes on a web page because it is difficult to select a unique one.

```
# Switch  to Iframes as Web Elements (Xpath)
# Switch to frame 1
driver.switch_to_frame("//iframe[@src='https://www.apress.com']")
```

```
# Switch to frame 2
driver.switch_to_frame("//iframe[@src='https://www.bing.com']")
```

```
# Switch to frame 3
driver.switch_to_frame("//iframe[@src='https://www.wikipedia.org']")
```

The iframes have been located using XPath, which is different for every frame.

Note   Since anchor tags are unavailable, link or partial link text is not used to switch an iframe.

Switching to a Main Iframe

There are two ways to switch to the main frame, which are discussed next.

Default Content

With default content, all available iframes are terminated, and the control is switched back to the web page. When the control is given back to the page, there is no interaction with the web elements present in an iframe.

```
driver.switch_to.default_content()
```

Parent Frame

With a parent frame, the current iframe is terminated, and the control is switched to its parent iframe. If there is no parent iframe corresponding to the selected or current iframe, then the current iframe is terminated, and the control is switched back to the web page.

```
driver.switch_to.parent_frame()
```

Frames with Waits

When handling iframes, you can use waits to switch to any frames because these frames take more time to load because of the external source or link. The following are a few examples of waits.

- Frame ID :

  ```
  iframe=WebDriverWait(driver, 5).until(EC.frame_to_be_available_
  and_switch_to_it(By.ID,"iframe_id"))
  ```

- Frame Name :

  ```
  iframe2 =WebDriverWait(driver, 5).until(EC.frame_to_be_available_
  and_switch_to_it(By.NAME,"iframe_name"))
  ```

- Frame XPath :

  ```
  iframe3 =WebDriverWait(driver, 5).until(EC.frame_to_be_available_
  and_switch_to_it(By.XPATH,"iframe_xpath"))
  ```

- Frame CSS :

  ```
  iframe4 =WebDriverWait(driver, 5).until(EC.frame_to_be_available_
  and_switch_to_it(By.CSS_SELECTOR,"iframe_css_selectors"))
  ```

Let's now move on to discuss textboxes.

Textboxes

A textbox accepts user input in the form of text. This text is stored in a database or used by the web page. There are two types of textboxes: single line and multiline.

Single-line Textbox

A single-line textbox is typically seen as login options, where the login and password each require a single line of text. The textbox is a rectangle shape on a single line; it comes in varied sizes. The input tag in HTML defines a single-line textbox. The following is an HTML example of a single-line textbox. It is shown in Figure 7-3.

```
<h1>Single Line Textbox</h1>
```

```
<label for="book">Book Name:</label>
<input type="text" id="book1" name="book">
```

Single Line Textbox

Book Name: Python Selenium

Figure 7-3. *Single-line textbox*

A single-line textbox is commonly used in forms or as a search box on a web page. The Google search engine is the most-used single-line textbox.

Multiline Textbox

When the text uses more than one line, then a multiline textbox is needed. A multiline textbox is often used for comment boxes on e-commerce sites or to post on Facebook. The size can vary with respect to rows and columns (height and width). To define a multiline textbox, the `<textarea>` tag is used. Figure 7-4 shows textarea and the text values in it. The following is the HTML code for it.

```
<h1>Textarea</h1>

<label for="book">Book Name:</label><br>

<textarea id="book2" cols="50" rows="5">
Python Selenium Sujay.
</textarea>
```

Textarea

Book Name:

```
Python Selenium Sujay.
```

Figure 7-4. *Multiline textBox*

The textarea can be dragged at the lower-right corner to increase its size. The size of the textarea can be restricted by specifying its corresponding parameters.

Note   A non-editable textbox is used only to display the values associated with it.

Inserting Values

The textbox and textarea are used to get values from the user. These values are stored in a database or verified against the values in the database to authorize or apply restrictions, accordingly. To test whether a textbox or textarea can receive input, you need to send values to it. This is done by using the send_keys function in Python with Selenium.

```
#Import libraries
from selenium import webdriver

#Open Firefox browser
driver=webdriver.Firefox()

#Navigate to URL
driver.get("http://www.apress.com")

#Find Search box (Single Line Textbox)
text_box=driver.find_element_by_name("query")

#String Value to be Inserted i.e. query in search box
text_box.send_keys("Python Testing with Selenium")

#Insert Value
text_box.submit()

# Quit Firefox
driver.quit()
```

Note   Inserting values in a textbox and textarea are largely the same; the only difference is the lines that incorporate them.

Getting Values from Textbox and Textarea

A test case can retrieve the input values given to a textbox or textarea. Any values concerning these boxes are retrieved to compare with an expected value, in case there is an error. The following is the Python code for a textbox and a textarea.

```
#For Textbox
text_box=driver.find_element_by_id('book1').get_property('value')
print(text_box)
```

```
#ForTextarea
text_area=driver.find_element_by_id('book2').get_property('value')
print(text_area)
```

Summary

This chapter briefly introduced iframes and the ways in which an iframe can be located. There are instances when multiple iframes are present on a web page. The process of switching to a specific iframe was explained with an example.

Textboxes are broadly classified as two types—single line and multiline. A multiline textbox is also known as a textarea. You learned to identify both types of textboxes using locators. You also learned about inserting values in both textbox types and retrieving the value associated with a specified textbox.

The next chapter is about validating web elements.

## CHAPTER 8

Assertions

In the preceding chapters, you studied locating web elements like links, buttons, frames, and textboxes, and the test cases related to them. Before automating any test case for a web app or page, you need to validate it, which is done by providing conditions about the web element. This validation or check is done by using assertion functions, which are available in Selenium with Python.

The assertion allows you to validate or check an expected value with the allocated value of the web elements. The allocated value may be any attribute associated with it, and the expected value is the one we compare in a test. This chapter explains the assertions provided by Python in Selenium with its types and usage to automate any test cases. These assertions are also part of the unittest framework, which is discussed in a later chapter of this book. In this chapter, we study several assertion methods that are provided by Selenium in Python, making debugging easier for test cases to be written.

The Need for Assertion

Assertion is a method primarily used to check or verify a specified condition or test case related to a web element. The assertion function or method gives two results: pass or fail (i.e., True or False in Boolean terms).

A test case passes only when two parameters or values in a test condition are the same, and no exception was raised during run time. Similarly, a test case fails when two values are not the same, and an AssertionError exception is raised (only when the assert function is used).

An assertion is mainly used to test a single web element in a test case, which is also called a *unit test*. It makes reports on the results of the related test case. The report informs developers about any errors or bugs associated with the test case.

The remaining sections organize assertion types by usage. Each type includes a brief definition, including syntax and example code.

© Sujay Raghavendra 2021

S. Raghavendra, *Python Testing with Selenium*, https://doi.org/10.1007/978-1-4842-6249-8_8

Basic Asserts

There are basic asserts provided by Python in Selenium that evaluate two values defined in it. The test case is successful or fails, depending on the results from the function. An exception is raised when a test case fails. An optional text message may also be provided.

assertTrue

`assertTrue` tests whether a given condition or result is true. A test case passes when a condition is true and fails when it is false. It verifies a single value, followed by a text message, which is optional. The following is an example of its syntax.

assertTrue(value1, text_msg=null)

```
import unittest
from selenium import webdriver

class test_case1(unittest.TestCase):
        def test1(self):
                s1 ="Python"
                s2 ="Ruby"

                # Verifying Numbers
                self.assertTrue(s1== s2, "It's not a Match.")
if __name__ =="__main__":
        unittest.main()
```

assertFalse

The `assertFalse` method passes a test when a specified condition is false.
A test fails when the condition is true, and an exception is raised. It uses a single value.
The following is an example of its syntax.

assertFalse(value1, text_msg=null)

```
def test2(self):
        s1 ="Python"

        # Verifying Numbers
        self.assertFalse(s1 == 'Ruby', "It's a Match.")
```

assertIs

The `assertIs` function matches value1 with value2 to see if they are the same or not. When two values are the same, the test case passes; otherwise, an exception is raised. The following is an example of its syntax.

```
assertIs(value1, value2, text_msg = null)

def test_lang(self):
        lang="Python"
        #Check lang
        self.assertIs("Selenium", lang, "value do not Match.")
```

assertIsNot

`assertIsNot` verifies whether value1 with value2 are the same or not. If they are not the same, then the test case passes; if they are the same, the test case fails. The following is an example of its syntax.

```
assertIsNot(value1, value2, text_msg = null)

def test_lang(self):
        lang="Python"
        #Check lang
        self.assertIsNot("Python", lang, "Value is Match.")
```

assertIsNone

`assertIsNone` checks whether the given condition or value is null. If null, then the test case passes; if it is not null, then the function raises an exception. The following is an example of its syntax.

```
assertIsNone(value, text_msg = null)
```

Here, value can be an expression or condition or parameter.

```
def test(self):
        color=None
                # Check if value is null.
                self.assertIsNone(color, "color is not null")
```

109

assertIsNotNone

The `assertIsNotNone` method passes a test case if the specified condition or value is not null; otherwise, the test case fails. The following is an example of its syntax.

```
assertIsNotNone(value, text_msg = null)
```

```
def test(self):
        color="green"
        # Check if value is not null.
        self.assertIsNotNone(color, "color is null")
```

assertIsInstance

`assertIsInstance` checks whether a given value is an instance of a class. An exception occurs if the object is not an instance. The following is an example of its syntax.

```
assertIsInstance(value, cls, text_msg = null)
```

assertNotIsInstance

`assertNotIsInstance` raises an exception when the given value is an instance of the class. If the value is not an instance of the class, then the corresponding test case passes. The following is an example of its syntax.

```
assertNotIsInstance(value, cls, text_msg = null)
```

Compare Assert

Assertion functions can be compared with each other. Two values are compared as greater or lesser by using the following assertions.

assertEqual

The assertEqual method compares two values. If the two values are equal, then the test case passes, and if they are not equal, then the test case fails to raise an exception. The pass and fail are in terms of the Boolean value returned by the function. The following is an example of its syntax.

assertEqual(value1, value2, text_msg=null)

The syntax defines two values for comparison, and a text message may be stated if both values do not match. The text message can be null, and hence, it is optional to use. The following is a simple example to test page title values (the executable path is the same as described in earlier chapters).

```python
import unittest
from selenium import webdriver

class test_case1(unittest.TestCase):
        def test1(self):
                driver=webdriver.Firefox()
                driver.get("https://apress.com")

                title1 =driver.title
                title2 ="Apress Home"

                # Verifying Page Title
                self.assertEqual(title1, title2, "Title Page do not Match.")

if __name__ =="__main__":
        unittest.main()
```

assertNotEqual

assertNotEqual acts contrast to the assertEqual function. A test case passes when two values are not equal; otherwise, test case fails. The following is an example of its syntax.

```python
assertNotEqual(value1, value2, text_msg=null)
def test2(self):
        num1 =7
        num2 =5
```

```
# Verifying Numbers
self.assertNotEqual(num1, num2, "Numbers Match.")
```

assertGreater

assertGreater checks whether the first value is greater than the second value; if yes, then the test passes, or else the test case is a failure. The following is an example of its syntax.

assertGreater (value1, value2, txt_msg = null)

assertGreaterEqual

The assertGreaterEqual function checks whether value1 is greater than or equal to value2; if yes, then the test case passes. The following is an example of its syntax.

assertGreaterEqual (value1, value2, txt_msg = null)

assertLess

With assertLess, a test case passes when value1 is less than value2, and the test case fails when value1 is less. A text message is optional. assertLess behaves opposite the assertGreater function. The following is an example of its syntax.

assertLess (value1, value2, txt_msg = null)

assertLessEqual

The assertLessEqual method passes the test case only when value1 is less than or equal to value2; otherwise, the test leads to failure with an exception raised. The following is an example of its syntax.

assertLessEqual (value1, value2, txt_msg = null)

```
def test_cmp(self):
    num1 =7
    num2 =5
```

```
#Check num1 is greater
self.assertGreater(num1, num2, "num1 is less.")

#Check num1 is greater than or equal to
self.assertGreaterEqual(num1, num2, "num1 is less.")

#Check num1 is less
self.assertLess(num1, num2, "num1 is greater.")

#Check num1 is less than or equal to
self.assertLessEqual(num1, num2, "num1 is greater.")
```

Collection Assert

Collections are special types of data storage where multiple elements can be stored. The collection includes list, tuples, set, dict, and so forth that are built in the Python language.

Lists

The assertListEqual function allows us to compare two lists. When both lists contain the same elements, then the test case passes; if lists do not have the same elements, then the test case fails. The following is an example of its syntax.

assertListEqual(list1, list2, text_msg=null)
```
def test_list(self):
        list1 = ["python", "selenium", "apress"]
        list2 = ["python", "selenium", "apress"]

        #Check elements in both lists
        self.assertListEqual(list1, list2, "Lists don't Match.")
```

Tuples

The comparison of elements is made between two tuples. When these two tuples have the same elements in them, then the function returns a Boolean value as True, which means that the test case passes and vice versa. The following is an example of its syntax.

assertTupleEqual(tuple1, tuple2, text_msg=null)

```python
def test_tuple(self):
        tuple1 = ("python", "selenium", "apress")
        tuple2 = ("python", "selenium", "apress")

        #Check elements between two tuples
        self.assertTupleEqual(tuple1, tuple2, "Tuples don't Match.")
```

Sets

Similar to the previous functions, the assertSetEqual function compares elements between two sets. If the two sets contain the same elements, then the test case passes or vice versa. The following is an example of its syntax.

assertSetEqual(set1, set2, text_msg=null)

```python
def test_set(self):
        set1 = {"python", "selenium", "apress"}
        set2 = {"java", "selenium", "apress"}

        #Check elements from two sets
        self.assertSetEqual(set1, set2, "Sets don't Match.")
```

Dictionary

In the assertDictEqual method, all the available elements from one dictionary are matched with another dictionary. If all elements are the same, then the test case is successful; if the elements are not the same, then the test case is a failure. The text message is optional. The following is an example of its syntax.

assertDictEqual(dict1, dict2, text_msg=null)

```python
def test_dict(self):
        dict1 = {"lang":"python", "tool":"selenium",
        "publication":"apress", "year":"2020"}
        dict2 = {"lang":"kotlin", "tool":"selenium",
        "publication":"apress", "year":"2020"}
```

```
#Check elements from two sets
self.assertDictEqual(dict1, dict2, "Dictionaries don't Match.")
```

assertIn

assertIn checks whether value1 is available in value2. If the value is available, then the test case passes without any exceptions. The following is an example of its syntax.

```
assertIn(value1, value2, text_msg = null)
```

Note   Collection assert is used to check availablility of web element from the collection.

assertNotIn

Like the assertIn function, assertNotIn checks whether value1 is present in value2. If it is present, then the test case fails; if it is not present, then the test case is a success. The following is an example of its syntax.

```
assertNotIn(value1, value2, text_msg = null)
```

The following program checks for an element's availability in any given collection data using the assertIn() and assertNotIn() functions.

```
def test_item(self):
        collection=set(["Python", "Selenium", "Apress"])

        #Check for Python element in a set
        self.assertIn("Python", collection, "Element is not available in
        the set.")
        #Check for Java element in a set
        self.assertNotIn("Java", collection, "Element is available in the set.")
```

Note   Some of the assertion functions have not been included because they are deprecated in the new version of Python.

This completes all the assertion functions that can be utilized in Python for a test case created using Selenium.

Summary

You learned about assertions in test cases. You also looked at different assertion techniques, such as basic asserts, compare asserts, and collection asserts with multiple functions.

The assertions explained in this chapter evaluate or validate the web elements present in a web application. Assertions allow you to make a report on debugging issues that occur in a test case so that developers can solve them quickly.

The next chapter discusses various exceptions in Selenium and ways to handle them.

CHAPTER 9

Exceptions

The last chapter discussed assertions, which evaluate a specified condition in a test case. This chapter focuses on exceptions that occur in Python with Selenium. First, you need to know what Selenium exceptions are and their various types. Several aspects raise exceptions in a Selenium test case. Each exception is caused by a specific reason, which is explained in this chapter. Selenium provides many built-in exceptions that later lead to the termination of a test case. To avoid these unusual terminations, an exception should be handled so that the test case follows the normal (default) execution flow. In this chapter, we study different types of exceptions, the causes that raise these exceptions, and how to handle exceptions in a Selenium test case. Let's start by defining exceptions and the need to have exceptions in a test case.

What Is an Exception?

An exception occurs when the execution of a program is interrupted by an unusual event. A test case stops its normal flow and is terminated when an exception is raised or occurs.

Why Use Exceptions?

The following are some of the reasons to use exceptions in Selenium.

- It separates the default test case code with error-handling code.

- There is no need to check errors at each point of the test case.

- An exception allows you to complete the default execution of a test case by any handling errors.

- It makes error reporting easier in a test case.

- Errors are easily classified when exceptions are used.

© Sujay Raghavendra 2021
S. Raghavendra, *Python Testing with Selenium*, https://doi.org/10.1007/978-1-4842-6249-8_9

Exceptions in Selenium

Now that you have considered the reasons to have exceptions in a test case, let's look at all the exceptions that can occur in Selenium when you execute a test case. Each exception is defined with the event that triggers the exception.

ConnectionClosedException

When a web driver is disconnected, Selenium raises this exception.

ElementClickInterceptedException

This exception occurs when a command to click an element is not executed correctly because the requested element that needs to be clicked is concealed or hidden.

ElementNotInteractableException

In this exception type, a defined web element cannot be interacted with or directs to another element, even if it is present in the Document Object Model (DOM).

ElementNotSelectableException

A web element cannot be selected, even when it is present in the DOM. This raises an exception. This action belongs to select in Selenium. The exception is more likely to occur in buttons to be slected like radio button, checkbox, etc.

ElementNotVisibleException

This exception is raised when an element is present on a web page, but it is not visible for actions to be performed on it. The invisibility of elements is due to a hidden type in an HTML tag, or some actions need to be performed first. This exception is solved by using a wait, which waits for an element to become visible.

ErrorInResponseException

This exception happens when there is an error on the server side. It is commonly seen when communicating with a remote server or a Firefox extension. The following lists some of these errors.

> 400 – BadRequest
>
> 401 – Unauthorized
>
> 403 – Forbidden
>
> 405 – MethodNotAllowed
>
> 409 – Conflict
>
> 500 – InternalServerError

ErrorHandler.UnknownServerException

When a server gives an error without a stack-trace, this exception is used as a placeholder.

ImeActivationFailedException

This exception is raised when the IME engine fails to activate. IME is the acronym for *input method engine*. It is generally used with Chinese, Japanese, or multibyte characters that are taken as input by Selenium. IBus is an example of an input framework that supports a Japanese engine like anthy.

ImeNotAvailableException

This exception occurs when IME support is not available on the device.

InsecureCertificateException

The TLS (Transport Layer Security) certificate, if expired or invalid, raises this exception at the user end.

InvalidArgumentException

When invalid or distorted arguments are passed, Selenium raises this exception.

InvalidCookieDomainException

Selenium invokes this exception when there is an effort to add a cookie for other domains or URLs rather than the present or current URL.

InvalidCoordinateException

This exception is activated when the defined coordinates are incorrect or invalid when the user needs to perform actions or operations on a corresponding web element. When mouse actions that move web elements or click buttons with provided coordinates fail, this exception is evoked.

InvalidElementStateException

When a web element is disabled or not in a state to perform the action specified to it, Selenium raises this exception. For example, the Submit button works when all the respective fields are filled, and if you try to click Submit beforehand, this exception is raised.

InvalidSelectorException

When users do not return specified web elements from the web page, InvalidSelectorException is raised. It is more likely to be raised by XPath because a path is invalid or changed, which means locating the web element fails.

InvalidSessionIdException

If a session ID in a test case is inactive, has expired, or does not exists, then Selenium raises this exception.

InvalidSwitchToTargetException

This exception occurs when a frame or window element is not available on a web page that needs to be placed or switched to a targeted location.

JavascriptException

If there is an issue regarding the execution of a JavaScript file or snippet, then this exception is invoked.

JsonException

This exception occurs when session capabilities are obtained when the session is not created.

MoveTargetOutOfBoundsException

When a target web element or mouse movement cannot be directed to the defined boundaries (i.e., beyond the boundary of the web page, or it is invalid), this exception is retained by ActionChains( ).

NoAlertPresentException

This exception happens when an alert popup (e.g., an alert box, prompt box, confirmation box, etc.) is not currently available. JavaScript guides the alert popup. Other reasons to raise this exception include an alert box requires more time to load or is unavailable at the current stage, JavaScript is blocked at the browser end, or the popup is already closed.

NoSuchAttributeException

If a web element is unable to return its attribute, then this exception is raised. It is one of the rarest Selenium exceptions that can occur in a test case. You can avoid this exception by knowing whether or not a web element has an attribute associated with it.

The exception can also be handled by updating the attribute value from the DOM that may have changed.

NoSuchCookieException

This exception is raised when there is no match for the cookie defined within the cookies present in the active document of the browser's current context.

NoSuchElementException

This is the most commonly occurring exception in Selenium WebDriver test cases. This exception is revoked when a web locator is unable to trace or locate the defined web element from a web page. The web element is not located because the DOM does not contain it, or it is invalid.

When the defined web element is not available on a web page, Selenium throws NoSuchElementFoundException. This exception may occurring do to any of the following reasons.

- The web element locator value is incorrect or does not match.

- The page takes a long time to load, so the web element is not located.

- The web element is unavailable or unseen on the web page at the time of test execution.

NoSuchElementException is handled by choosing a specific web locator from eight available locators (see Chapter 4 for more information). It also specifies wait to ensure that the web element has completely loaded.

NoSuchFrameException

This exception occurs when you want to switch to a frame that is currently unavailable. This happens when the specific details to switch the frame changes while refreshing the page, or the information does not match any of the frames available, or the web element is not a frame, or loading time is insufficient.

NoSuchWindowException

When certain actions should be performed in a browser window (like switch to a defined window or move the window's position), this exception is raised if the window is not currently present. It also occurs when the window has not yet loaded and actions are attempted on it.

NoSuchContextException

In mobile testing, ContextAware evokes this exception.

ScreenshotException

This exception happens when Selenium fails to take a screenshot of the web page. The exception, when raised, turns the screenshot into a black image.

StaleElementReferenceException

This exception occurs when a web element is no longer present in the DOM because it was deleted or in a stable state. It is common because most web elements are now dynamic. A simple example is that a refreshing page may result in the unavailability of the defined web element.

This exception can be handled by XPath, which handles dynamic web elements on a web page.

TimeoutException

When the execution is not completed within the defined time frame, Selenium returns a timeout exception. The exception is handled using waits that enable you to provide more time for execution. The time value should be standard so that there is no delay in the further execution of the test case.

UnableToSetCookieException

This exception is raised when Selenium WebDriver is not able to set a cookie.

UnexpectedAlertPresentException

Selenium raises this alert when an unexpected alert appears on a web page, which is due to stalling Python commands from alerts (i.e., popups) .

UnexpectedTagNameException

This exception happens when the expected web element is unable to be located or found by the support class. It more commonly occurs in drop-down elements.

UnknownMethodException

This exception is raised when the requested Selenium commands match the known URL but fail to match the methods specified for the URL. To avoid this exception, you need to check the method before stating it in a test case.

WebDriverException

This is a base class Selenium WebDriver exception that is invoked when there is an incompatibility between WebDriver and the target web browser. All other exceptions come under this base class.

Exception Handling

Now that you know all the exceptions that occur in a Selenium test case, let's examine the proper ways to handle them. The process to continue the execution of a test case after an exception is raised is known as *exception handling* or *handling exceptions*. Exceptions are handled to execute and avoid the unnecessary termination of a test case.

Exceptions hamper the next valid statements that need to be executed, and hence, Selenium provides a solution to handle exceptions. An exception can be handled by skipping or ignoring the raised exception, and thus, the test case continues to execute in its normal flow.

Note   Handling exceptions reduces debugging time.

An exception is handled using the try-except method in Python. By defining an exception, you can ignore or skip it when it appears during test case execution. Exception handling helps to reduce false failures in a test case and leads to finding actual bugs, if any. Some common examples of exception handling in test cases are discussed next.

Timeout Exception

The web element locator waits for a specified time so that there is a provision to load the complete page.

```python
from selenium import webdriver
from selenium.webdriver.support.ui import WebDriverWait
from selenium.webdriver.support import expected_conditions as EC
from selenium.common.exceptions import TimeoutException
from selenium.webdriver.common.by import By
driver=webdriver.Firefox(executable_path=r'C:\folder\geckodriver.exe)
driver.get("https://apress.com")

try:
        # Web driver waits for 5 seconds to locate web element
        WebDriverWait(driver,5).until(EC.presence_of_element_located
        ((By.ID, "query")))

except TimeoutException:
        # When loading page takes more time
        print("Taking more time to load.")
```

Element Not Found

This is one of the most common exceptions that occurs in Python with Selenium.

```python
from selenium import webdriver
from selenium.common.exceptions import NoSuchElementException
from selenium.webdriver.common.action_chains import ActionChains

driver=webdriver.Firefox()
driver.get("https://apress.com")

try:
            web1 =driver.find_element_by_id("privacy")
        web1.click()

except NoSuchElementException as exception:
        print ("Web Element is not Available in the given Web Page.")
```

Stale Element

A stale element occurs when the web element is no longer present in the DOM. This exception is raised in the following program by submitting the web element after a while of its first submission. The handled exception is ignored or skipped that tries to terminate a test case. Similarly any exception can be handled. The same method can also be used for multiple exceptions that may occur in a test case.

```python
from selenium import webdriver
from selenium.common.exceptions import StaleElementReferenceException
import time
driver= webdriver.Firefox(')
driver.get('http://apress.com')

driver.find_element_by_name('query').send_keys('python selenium')

while True:
        try:
                        s=driver.find_element_by_class_name('search__submit')
                s.submit()
                time.sleep(2)
                s.submit()
        except StaleElementReferenceException:
                print('Stale Exception is Skipped.')
        break
driver.quit()
```

Note   Each exception in Selenium is handled in the same way that it is handled in Python (i.e., using the try-except method).

The exception handles the ignores or skips that terminate a test case. Any exception can be handled. The same method can also be used for multiple exceptions that may occur in a test case.

Summary

This chapter introduced and defined Selenium exceptions. You learned about the reasons to have Selenium exceptions in a test case.

Nearly all the exceptions that can occur in a Selenium test case were defined, and the reasons for their occurrence during test execution were explained. In the last section, you studied handling the most common exceptions in an example test case.

The next chapter discusses waits, in which a test case is delayed for a specified amount of time.

CHAPTER 10

Waits

Chapter 9 was about the various exceptions that could occur in a test case, and you saw how to handle them. This chapter provides a brief introduction to the waits that are used in Python on Selenium. A wait can minimize most of the exceptions that are triggered during the run of a test case.

There are times when web elements are available after specific actions are performed or after some time interval. These actions are done on the user end through forms, buttons, or mouse/keyboard actions that navigate or redirect the user to another web page.

The actions can also be performed using AJAX, which is a combination of JavaScript and language (hence the acronym comes from Asynchronous JavaScript and XML). The availability or visibility of web elements is controlled using AJAX or JavaScript in the code. The extensive use of AJAX or JavaScript is because it

- Updates a web app/page without loading it again

- Requests server data after loading the page

- Receives server data after loading the page

- Sends data to a server without refreshing/loading the page again

The need for waits is explained next.

Note   AJAX can send or receive data in plain text or JSON text.

© Sujay Raghavendra 2021
S. Raghavendra, *Python Testing with Selenium*, https://doi.org/10.1007/978-1-4842-6249-8_10

Why the Need for Waits?

Most web apps/pages are made with AJAX or JavaScript by using frameworks like AngularJS, NodeJS, ReactJS, and so forth. These apps load web elements on a page by refreshing (reloading) the page or loading it. To locate such web elements, Selenium provides waits.

Python scripts are written to automate a user's interactions. Consider a simple example: when a form is filled, and the Submit button is clicked, the page is redirected. The web elements are available after the submission is made. Hiding web elements is done using JavaScript or AJAX. To make these web elements visible, you must wait for a specific action to be performed or a page to load. Any errors or exceptions raised cannot be resolved because the elements are hidden. Selenium waits are essentially used to overcome these kinds of errors that occur when redirecting web applications. Waits also handle the number of exceptions by locating web elements.

There following are a few of the many reasons why a web element cannot be located.

- All the web elements have not completely loaded on the web page due to a variation in time when AJAX or JavaScript is used.

- The web elements are made available only when there is a specified action performed by the user.

- There is a delay in the response to the web page.

- The web page/application behaves adversely, and the web elements fail to load.

Types of Waits

Waits handle exceptions like ElementNotVisibleException and NoSuchElementException from Selenium WebDriver. The waits are defined by conditions to locate the web elements on a web page. Depending on the conditions, the waits are typically classified into three types by Selenium WebDriver: implicit, explicit, and fluent.

Implicit

In an implicit wait, the WebDriver is made to wait (poll DOM) for a specified amount of time before invoking the NoSuchElementFound exception. The default time for the wait is zero seconds. It can be implemented on any web elements available on the page.

Note   DOM stands for Document Object Model, which is an interface for HTML and XML.

The wait condition is defined in a Python script that looks for the presence of a specified web element on a given page. WebDriver does not proceed until the web element is found within the set time frame in the condition script. If the element is not found within the set time, an exception is raised.

The concept of waiting for a web element is taken from the Watir tool. Listing 10-1 shows an example of an implicit wait. (Please note that paths are explained in Chapters 1 and 2.)

Listing 10-1. Implicit Wait

```
# Import Selenium Libraries
from selenium import webdriver
from selenium.webdriver.common.keys import Keys

# Time frame set for 10 seconds
timeout =10

# Creating Firefox driver instance
driver = webdriver.Firefox()

# Calling Implicit wait function
driver.implicitly_wait(timeout) #driver.implicitly_wait(10) Time frame can
diretly be set

# Go to URL www.apress.com
driver.get("http://apress.com")

print("It's an Implicit Wait")
```

```python
# Retrieving ID element
new_element = driver.find_element_by_id("query")

# Type "Python with selenium" in search bar
new_element.send_keys("Python with selenium")

# Submit text in search bar
new_element.submit()

# Close Firefox browser
driver.quit()
```

In this example, the web driver is made to wait for 10 seconds to find/locate the web element by ID. The tester determines the time frame. The web driver tries to search the specified element in the defined time frame; if found, the web driver returns the element, the prescribed text is submitted, and the browser is closed. If an element is not found, then an exception is raised.

Note   An implicit wait is used for web elements that are not instantly available.

Explicit

The web elements on a page are loaded or made available after specific conditions are met. These conditions may vary from element to element. In such cases, the implicit wait cannot be used because it can only wait until an element is loaded or appears. The wait time cannot be increased drastically, which may lead to more time to execute the whole script. This leads to the use of an improved version of the implicit wait, which is called an *explicit wait*.

Consider a dynamic web page having an element that can only be loaded after user interaction. If an implicit wait is used, it waits for a specified time and then throws an exception because the element is not present or visible. Explicit waits are used to locate these elements. The explicit wait, when used, defines two conditions: WebDriver wait and ExpectedConditions in the Python class.

The first condition, a WebDriver wait, defines an integer value that waits a certain amount of time. The second condition defines ExpectedConditions for the specified web element. The ExpectedConditions are predefined functions/methods available in the Selenium WebDriver Python library. When the ExpectedConditions are met, then WebDriver does not wait for the defined wait to complete and proceeds to the next code instruction in the Python script. This is the major difference between implicit and explicit waits.

Note   The default poll frequency of an explicit wait is 500 milliseconds (0.5 seconds) and cannot be altered.

Listing 10-2. Explicit Wait

```python
# Import all Necessary Selenium Libraries
from selenium import webdriver
Missing python timeout exception
from selenium.webdriver.support.ui import WebDriverWait
from selenium.webdriver.support import expected_conditions as EC
from selenium.webdriver.common.keys import Keys
from selenium.webdriver.common.by import By
from selenium.common.exceptions import TimeoutException

# Creating Firefox driver instance
driver = webdriver.Firefox()

# Go to URL www.apress.com
driver.get("https://www.apress.com")

# Time frame set for 10 seconds
timeout =10

try:

# Returns ID element, when successful
        new_element = WebDriverWait(driver,timeout).until(
        EC.presence_of_element_located((By.ID, "query")))

# Type "Python with selenium" in search bar
    new_element.send_keys("Python with selenium")

# Submitting text in search bar
```

```
    new_element.send_keys(Keys.ENTER)
except TimeoutException:
        print("Failed to locate search bar")

finally:
    driver.quit()

# Closing Firefox browser
driver.quit()
```

In Listing 10-2, the time frame is set for 10 seconds. The driver visits the Apress web page, where its ID attribute locates an element. The web element is checked for the specified time and returns if available; otherwise, an exception is encountered. So, if a loop is used, it may take an infinite amount of time until the condition is satisfied. The loop fails when there is a page redirect. When the wait is set, it checks at regular intervals and comes out of the flow when the element is located or the time ends.

Note   Mixing both implicit and explicit waits can lead to an infinite waiting period.

Explicit waits use the ExpectedConditions necessary to locate web elements. Each of these conditions is described next.

Commonly Used ExpectedConditions in the Python Class

ExpectedConditions commonly automate a script for testing. These conditions are encountered regularly and are primarily used in an explicit wait.

ExpectedConditions are predefined in Python in the Selenium package library. You need to install and import the Python script before incorporating it. ExpectedConditions are available in the expected_condition module. The Python script to import the library file is from selenium.webdriver.support import expected_conditions as ec.

Note   ec is a shortened form of expected_conditions, which is generally used in the Python language.

ExpectedConditions are for web elements. The following describes the ExpectedConditions that are commonly used to automate tests.

- **alert_is_present**

  It checks whether an alert is present on a web page or not within a specified time frame. If present, it returns the alert object; otherwise, it raises Selenium common exceptions like TimeoutException.

- **element_located_selection_state_to_be(ui_locator, is_selected)**

  It checks if a web element can be located by any of the locators on a web page and checks its state of selection. If a specified web element is found with its desired selection state within a set time frame, then no exception is raised.

- **element_located_to_be_selected(ui_locator)**

  It checks if a web element is in a selected state on a web page within the time frame. The element can be located using any of the locators mentioned in Chapter 4. Exceptions are raised when elements are not found.

- **element_selection_state_to_be(ui_element, is_selected)**

  It is similar to **element_located_selection_state_to_be**; the only difference is that in this case, a web element is passed instead of a locator identifying it. It also checks for the state of the element identified before returning it.

- **element_to_be_clickable(ui_locator)**

  In this case, the web element should be in an invisible state that allows a click mechanism on it. This exception condition waits until the set time and tries to locate the specified clickable web element using locators. If no element with a click is encountered, then an exception is invoked.

- **element_to_be_selected(ui_element)**

  It checks if a web element is in a selected state. It is like **element located to be selected**, but in this method, the element is in a selected state by directly passing the web element in place of a locator. The exception is raised when the element is not found within the set time limit.

- **frame_to_be_available_and_switch_to_it(ui_locator)**

  It checks for the specified frame on the web page within the set time and switches to it. If the frame is present, then the given driver is switched to this frame, or it raises a timeout exception.

- **invisibility_of_element_located(ui_locator)**

  It checks if the specified element is visible/invisible in the DOM in the defined time. This element can be either a locator or a web element. When the web element is invisible or is removed from the DOM, there is a No Timeout or a No Such Element exception.

- **title_is(title)**

  It checks if the specified text is in the title of the web page. The text is case sensitive. The text must be an exact match with the title of the web page; otherwise, it returns a timeout exception.

- **staleness_of(ui_element)**

  This method waits until an element is no longer associated with the DOM. The web element has become old or has been deleted from the DOM because a part of or the entire page, or only the element has been refreshed, which is known as a *stale element* in Selenium. If the stale element is not found, then it returns a Boolean value as False.

- **text_to_be_present_in_element(ui_locator, inner_text)**

  It checks if the specified text is present in the identified or located web element. Here, the locator finds the element and then checks for text. If text is present in the element, then no exception is raised.

- **text_to_be_present_in_element_value(ui_locator, value)**

  It checks if the text is present in the element's value attribute within the time frame. If it is not present, then one of two exceptions (i.e., Timeout or NoSuchElement) is raised.

- **title_contains(title_text)**

  It checks if the specified text is present in the title of a web page. If some or all of the specified text is present in the web page title, then the matched page title is returned. The text is case sensitive.

- **visibility_of(ui_element)**

  It checks whether a web element in the DOM page is visible or not. Here, visibility means that the element not only has a height and width greater than 0 (zero) but also if the element is displayed.

  This method checks whether a web element is in a hidden state on the DOM page, or if it is made visible to the user by a timeout or user interaction. An exception is raised if the element is not visible.

- **visibility_of_all_elements_located(ui_locator)**

  It checks if all web elements are present in the DOM and visible. The elements should be displayed with height and weight greater than zero. It returns all located visible web elements; otherwise, an exception is raised.

  Consider a web page with seven elements in it; only four are visible, and the other three are in a hidden state. In this case, the web driver waits for the other three elements to be visible in the allotted duration of time. If the elements do not switch to a visible state from a hidden state, then the timeout exception is raised.

- **visibility_of_any_elements_located(ui_locator)**

  It checks if at least one element is registered in the DOM and visible on the web page. The visibility criteria are the same; for example, in a web page with five web elements present in the DOM and visible. The WebDriver tries to locate one among three to satisfy the expected condition. An exception is raised if none are visible or registered in the DOM.

- **visibility_of_element_located(ui_locator)**

  It checks for an element that is traced by locator and is registered in DOM as well as visible, respectively. The web element is displayed and has dimensions (i.e., height and weight) more than zero.

- **invisibility_of_element_located(ui_locator)**

  It checks that a web element is neither present in DOM nor visible on a web page. This is a contrast condition of **visibility_of_element_located(ui_locator)**. When an element is still visible and does not switch to a hidden state within the time limit set, then the exception is raised.

- **new_window_is_opened(current_handles)**

  It is a condition in which a new window is opened, and the number of window handles is increased.

- **number_of_windows_to_be(num_windows)**

  It checks if the number of windows has a certain value. This value is an integer defined in the given method. When the value matches the number of windows, then no exception is raised.

- **url_changes(url)**

  In this condition, the current URL (Uniform Resource Locator) is changed by the new URL (i.e., the expected one). When the URL of the web page changes, then this condition is used. Both the current and expected URLs should not be the same. If the current URL is not changed, then an exception is raised. The URL is case sensitive.

- **url_contains(url)**

  The defined URL string is checked to see whether the current URL contains any part of it or not. If it matches the substring, then no exceptions are invoked. The string is case sensitive.

- **url_matches(url)**

  It checks the current URL with the defined URL string. This condition checks for the exact pattern in the current URL. If the pattern is detected, then the exception is not invoked. The pattern may be a regular expression.

- **url_to_be(url)**

  It checks the current URL against the expected one. It is like URL_**matches(url)** method, but the only difference is that this method uses the actual URL, which is not in a regular expression format. The current URL should be an exact match with the expected one, or else an exception is raised.

- **presence_of_all_elements_located(locator)**

  It checks for the presence of at least one element in a web page that is identified using locators. Multiple web elements on the same web page can be present, which are matched by locators. If the list of matched web elements is returned, no exception is raised. The number of matched elements is done within a time frame.

- **presence_of_element_located(locator)**

  It checks whether a web element is available on a web page DOM. The availability of elements on the DOM is not necessarily visible. The locator finds the element. An exception is raised when an element is not present on the DOM.

Note   The expected conditions are set within a time frame; if the condition is not met, then the timeout exception is invoked. The time constraint can be customized if the element is present.

Differences Between Implicit and Explicit

Now that you've reviewed implicit and explicit waits, let's look at the distinctions between them, as provided in Table 10-1.

Table 10-1. *Difference Between Implicit and Explicit Waits*

Implicit	Explicit
It can be applied to all available web elements on a web page/app	Only applies to elements that the user interacts with
ExpectedConditions cannot be defined	ExpectedConditions need to be defined
Elements are located only by waiting for a specified time	ExpectedConditions are checked for the set time to locate elements
The specified time cannot be ignored	When ExpectedConditions are met, then the remaining time is ignored

Fluent

A fluent wait sets both the waiting period and the poll frequency of a web element. The web element is checked regularly to locate within the set time frame. The poll frequency and time frame can vary as desired. A fluent wait tries to trace/locate a web element at regular intervals for a specified time frame or until the element is found.

A fluent wait is useful in cases where web elements using AJAX take longer than usual or become visible within a shorter time interval. It allows you to ignore any exceptions. The exceptions are specified with time interval and poll frequency. A simple Python script of a fluent wait is given in Listing 10-3.

> **Note**   Fluent waits are recommended for real-time web apps because polling gets the updated results.

Listing 10-3. Fluent Wait

```
# Import all Necessary Selenium Libraries
from selenium import webdriver
from selenium.webdriver.support.ui import WebDriverWait
from selenium.webdriver.support import expected_conditions as EC
from selenium.webdriver.common.by import By
```

```
from selenium.common.exceptions import ElementNotVisibleException
from selenium.common.exceptions import ElementNotSelectableException

# Creating Firefox driver instance
driver = webdriver.Firefox()

# Go to URL www.apress.com
driver.get("https://www.apress.com")

# Time frame set for 10 seconds
timeout =10

# Fluent Wait with time interval, poll frequency and exceptions
wait = WebDriverWait(driver, timeout,
        poll_frequency=1,
        ignored_exceptions=[ElementNotVisibleException,
        ElementNotSelectableException])

# Retrieving ID element
new_element = wait.until(EC.presence_of_element_located((By.ID, "query")))

# Close Firefox browser
driver.quit()
```

A fluent wait with a time frame of 10 seconds and a poll frequency is set to one that checks for web element with its ID stated at each second until a timeout occurs as in program 3. Exceptions like NoSuchElementExceptions and ElementNotVisibleException are also ignored if raised, and finally, the browser is closed.

Note   A poll frequency in fluent waits can be customized.

Summary

Waits provide a genuine solution to issues with page refresh/loading and the untimely occurrence of web elements in a web application. This chapter explained the different types of waits (implicit, explicit, and fluent) supported by Selenium.

An implicit wait provides a time frame to locate a specified web element in a web application. An explicit wait has a time frame and ExpectedConditions; either is validated to meet the defined condition. The ExpectedConditions present in an explicit wait are also explained in detail. Finally, the fluent wait was explored in an example. The fluent wait is an improved version among waits because it supports time limits, poll frequency, and an exception can be ignored in its function.

A model is required to integrate all the various test cases that we have learned till now. This model is built on page objects. The next chapter covers topics on page objects and models related to it.

CHAPTER 11

Page Objects

In all the previous chapters, you learned to write various test conditions for the web elements present in a web page. A test case is built by combining these conditions. Building a successful test case requires a model in which all the essential functions and methods are integrated into a single test case or script. When test cases are bundled into a single script, the complexity of the test script increases, which makes it difficult to read, modify, or maintain. Page objects are used to solve jumbled-up test script issues on a web page.

The chapter begins with the discussion of page objects. The later sections cover the most widely used model for automating tests. The chapter also describes the necessity of the model in today's environment. Further, you learn the complete process for building a model based on page objects, which is a widely used testing model. This model is defined in a classic example in this chapter. The Selenium support for the model also helps with encapsulating a test case. Now let's start with page objects overview.

Page Objects Overview

Page objects are classes (an object-oriented concept in Python) that are initialized for a web page. A page object has web elements defined within it, like attributes in the Python language. The page object class serves as a medium to store web elements with their actions and the validations associated with the web page/app. Web elements can be easily accessed using page objects. Multiple page objects can be defined in a Python test script, depending on the requirements.

The basic concept of a page object is to hide the logic to locate the web elements (i.e., user ID, XPath, CSS selectors, etc.) that interact with these elements on a web page when a value is entered, which separates logic and value fields.

© Sujay Raghavendra 2021
S. Raghavendra, *Python Testing with Selenium*, https://doi.org/10.1007/978-1-4842-6249-8_11

Note   Page objects are best suited for web applications with more than one page.

Now let's look at a model that is built using page objects.

Page Object Model (POM) Overview

In test automation, a design pattern or model has emerged that allows more functionality, maintainability, readability, and flexibility. This design model/pattern based on page objects is known as a Page Object Model (POM) or Page Object Pattern.

(These terms are used interchangeably, but this book uses only POM.)

Page objects are better than unstructured Selenium test scripts and are well-suited for simple test cases/scenarios. As test cases increase in multiple web pages, the complexity of a test script also increases. To bind test cases together and to simplify the test script, a design model or pattern using page objects was developed.

POM in the Selenium WebDriver testing domain was proposed by Simon Steward. The first implementation of the Page Object Model was done in Java, which was later adopted by C#, Ruby, and then Python because they all supported object-oriented concepts.

POM is an organized way to automate Python test scripts. It contains the web elements that have user actions or interactions associated with them and that are tested, which means that POM provides encapsulation for the page objects.

Initially, page objects were defined for each web page, but due to the dynamic nature of web elements, objects can also be defined as classes or functions in a Python test case. In recent years, the use of page objects has increased in Selenium's automated testing.

Note   A page object is also used for important web elements available in a single web page or application despite the term *page object*.

The Need for the Page Objects Model

Each web page or specialized web elements, when represented as a class, then a page object serves as an interface medium between page and AUT. The methods described in the class are the test case that interacts with a web page UI when executed.

A major reason to use a POM is that changes in a web page's UI do not affect test cases. Change is handled by modifying the page objects related to it, which prevents the time and effort of writing a new test.

The procedural way that the model is implemented is explained next.

Creating Page Objects

A page object model is divided into various modules. These test modules contain a main test page that links to other module files. The modules are related to elements, locators, and pages for the specified test case.

A sample POM test case is provided next, where test.py is the main test case file followed by subsidiary files: page.py, elements.py, and locators.py. All files are kept in a single directory.

To execute the POM, you need to run test.py in the command prompt, and each subsidiary file is executed one by one when it is called.

Let's now create each page necessary to form the POM, starting with the test.py file.

Test.py

test.py is a test case that is developed using the POM architecture. The test.py page contains all the test cases that are necessary to test a specific web page or application. In this example, the POM is designed to test searching a keyword on the Apress web site and then get matching results. test.py needs to import the associated modules, called the page.py file, to complete the test case.

Keep all four files in a single directory. Don't run them individually because it is the Page Object Model, which is similar to the Page Object Pattern in Java.

```python
import unittest
from selenium import webdriver
import page

class ApressSearch(unittest.TestCase):
#Sample test case using Page Object Model

def setUp(self):
        self.driver = webdriver.Firefox(executable_path=r'')
        self.driver.get("https://www.apress.com")
```

```
def test_apress_search(self):
#Visits aprèss.com
        home_page = page.HomePage(self.driver)

#Searches "Python Selenium" keyword
        home_page.search_text ="Python Selenium"
        home_page.click_submit_button()
        search_results_page = page.ResultPage(self.driver)

        #Checks if page is not empty
        assert search_results_page.check_search_results(), "No results
        found."

def tearDown(self):
        self.driver.close()

if __name__ =="__main__":
    unittest.main()
```

The test.py file visits the specified web site (Apress.com) and then searches for "Python Selenium" via the search box. The resulting page is also verified, whether it's empty or not, with an assertion.

Note   The test.py file contains only test cases.

Page.py

The page.py file is created for each web page available in an application. In this file, the actions concerning the test cases are defined. This page separates the test code and its implementation on technical aspects. The page should import elements and locator files along with the standard Selenium library.

```
from elements import BasePageElement
from locators import HomePageLocators

class SearchText(BasePageElement):
```

```
#The locator for search box where search string is entered
    locator ='query'

class BasePage(object):

        def __init__(self, driver):
                self.driver = driver

class HomePage(BasePage):
        #Actions items for Home Page

        #Variable containing retrieved text
        search_text = SearchText()

        def click_submit_button(self):
        #Search is initialized
                element=self.driver.find_element(*HomePageLocators.SUBMIT_
                BUTTON)
                element.click()

classResultPage(BasePage):
#Actions items for result page

        def check_search_results(self):
        # Checks the result for specified text if found or not
        return "No results found." not in self.driver.page_source
```

The Submit button click action is defined on this page. It verifies whether the search page result is available or not.

Elements.py

elements.py contains a class that is initialized for each page. This page finds the necessary web elements that are associated with functions performing actions. It can also set conditions to locate web elements.

```python
from selenium.webdriver.support.ui import WebDriverWait

class BasePageElement(object):
#Used in every page
        def __set__(self, obj, value):
        #Contains specified text
                driver = obj.driver
                WebDriverWait(driver, 100).until(lambda driver: driver.
                find_element_by_name(self.locator))
                driver.find_element_by_name(self.locator).clear()
                        driver.find_element_by_name(self.locator).send_
                        keys(value)

        def __get__(self, obj, owner):
"""Gets the text of the specified object"""
                driver = obj.driver
                WebDriverWait(driver, 100).until(
lambda driver: driver.find_element_by_name(self.locator))
                element = driver.find_element_by_name(self.locator)
                return element.get_attribute("value")
```

In this page, the web elements are located after waiting for a defined time, and then they are provided to test.py through the page.py file.

Locators.py

The locators.py page contains the names of the web elements that need to be located. This separates pages from elements and locators. Any changes in locator values are done in this page.

```python
from selenium.webdriver.common.by import By

class HomePageLocators(object):
        #Should contain all locators from main page
        SUBMIT_BUTTON = (By.CLASS_NAME, 'search__submit')

class ResultPageLocators(object):
        #It should contain locators from result page
        pass
```

The locators initialized are passed to elements.py, where it locates web elements for the specified page. The POM is sometimes considered a framework to deploy test cases with Selenium using Python. A test case framework known as unittest is combined with POM. It is described in Chapter 12.

Advantages of Page Objects Model

This section focuses on the advantages of test cases that are created with page objects, as follows.

- **Reduces code duplication:** The basic test scripts required by most of the web page undergoing testing needs to be rewritten, which creates duplication of code. This code duplication can be avoided by using page objects because the same test script has page objects specified for various web elements and can be used for other pages.

- **Enhances code maintenance:** The creation of a page class helps to separate web elements (data) and test cases. This enables you to avoid unstable test suite conditions in a changing environment. The handling of exceptions in a test case means a more maintainable test script.

- **Shorter test cases:** The test script is optimized using POM, and hence the length of test cases is reduced.

- **Increases code reusability:** Code that uses page objects can be used in multiple test cases.

- **Readability:** The test script written for any web application should be understandable to a new tester or multiple test teams working on the same project. This is done by using page objects that divide the web elements or web pages into several parts, which makes the test script more readable.

Limitations of the Page Object Model

Let's now look at the limitations of using page objects in a test case.

- **Time and effort:** There is a huge risk with using page objects when a web page or application has a large number of pages because the test model needs to be modified for even minor changes in an application. Hence, POM should be used in parallel with the development of the web application/page.

- **High-level skills:** To debug or to write test cases aligned to POM, you must have technical knowledge and experience because complexity increases with combined page object architectures.

- **Fixed model:** A test developed with POM cannot be utilized on other applications (i.e., POM is not a generic model).

Summary

This chapter provided a complete overview of the page objects that build a model. Page objects are classes that divide a web page into smaller sections, which distinguishes the multiple web elements available in them. It is the basic building block to create the model.

You learned the conceptual and technical implementation aspects of the Page Object Model. The creation of POM includes a file structure that has a main Python file and subsidiary Python files that reside in a single directory, as demonstrated in an example.

You also learned POM's advantages and limitations.

The final chapter of this book includes various test cases written using different functions.

CHAPTER 12

Using Test Cases with a Screenshot

The program in Python on Selenium that tests a specified element on a web application or web page is called a *test case*. Selenium with Python is a popular choice for testing a web application or web page because there is a lower learning curve to implement it. Python is an easy-to-understand language. Testing requires you to generate simple, understandable test reports for a web application, which can be done with Python and Selenium combined.

This chapter discusses the various test cases used to take a screenshot. In the previous chapter, you learned how POM creates a test case.

Let's now study the most widely used framework supported by Python in Selenium. The framework implementation as a test case for a web page is also discussed. First, let's quickly review the test outcomes.

Test Outcomes

The test code has three outcomes: pass, fail, or error. These outcomes define the changes that need to be provided in a test case. The following offers a quick description.

Pass/OK

Pass/OK is the outcome that a developer usually expects. It means that the application is ideal and errorless in terms of functionality and client satisfaction. It is achieved by rigorously testing the web page or application. When a test passes, the application does not need any changes or bug fixes.

© Sujay Raghavendra 2021
S. Raghavendra, *Python Testing with Selenium*, https://doi.org/10.1007/978-1-4842-6249-8_12

Fail

A test fails when a test condition is not satisfied in the corresponding web elements or its behavior. When a test case fails, an AssertionError exception is raised by the system. This error is stated to the developer to make the necessary changes, which are also tested.

Error

An error occurs when an exception is raised. The error may be due to logic, syntax, or semantics and can be traced by the raised exception. This exception is not an AssertionError.

Let's now look at a few test cases in which the same goal is achieved using multiple approaches.

Test Case 1: Taking a Screenshot

This test case takes a picture (i.e., screenshot) of the web page. The size of the screenshot is determined by specifying the height and width. This is useful in bug analyses reports, for seeing the test case flow, and in recovering failed test cases.

Three methods can be used to capture screen images in Selenium. Each one is described next.

save_screenshot ('name_of_file')

In this method, the screenshot is taken during the execution of a test case. The screenshot image is available in a .png extension. The following is the Python code for it.

```
from selenium import webdriver

new_driver=webdriver.Firefox()
new_driver.get('https://apress.com')

new_driver.save_screenshot('screenshot1.png')
```

get_screenshot_as_file ('name_of_file')

This method directly saves the screenshot as image in .png format. Any other image extension apart from .png throws an error. The following is the Python code for it.

```
#get_screenshot_as_file()
from selenium import webdriver

driver=webdriver.Firefox()
driver.get('https://apress.com')

driver.get_screenshot_as_file('screenshot2.png')

#Error Occurs when image extension is changed
#driver.get_screenshot_as_file('screenshot2.jpg')
```

get_screenshot_as_png()

In this method type, the screenshot is captured in binary form, which is then converted to an image. The saved image is stored in .png format. The following is the Python code for it.

```
#Get method
from selenium import webdriver
from PIL import Image
from io import BytesIO

driver= webdriver.Firefox(executable_path=r'C:\Users\ADMIN\Desktop\
geckodriver.exe')
driver.get('http://apress.com/')

#Logo Image extraction
element=driver.find_element_by_class_name('brand')
location=element.location

#saves logo image as screenshot
size=element.size
png=driver.get_screenshot_as_png()
driver.quit()
```

```
#PIL library is used to open image in memory
image=Image.open(BytesIO(png))

#Logo size extraction
left= location['x']
top= location['y']
right= location['x'] + size['width']
bottom= location['y'] + size['height']

#Saving Logo for extracted dimension size
image=image.crop((left, top, right, bottom))
image.save('C:\\Users\\ADMIN\Desktop\\python books\\#Go Lang\\Done\\final\
Apress\python testing\\codes\\screenshot3.png')
```

The Python Imaging Library (PIL) Library is used for converting a binary image. It is available in Python. The size of the image is specified before implementing this function.

Note   In Python on Selenium, the save_screenshot () and get_screenshot_as_file () methods can only store the image in .png format, whereas the get_screenshot_as_png () method can store the image in multiple formats.

Now we'll look at the testing frameworks and the most popular testing framework used in Selenium implementation.

Testing Frameworks

A test case is governed by a set of rules and regulations, which is done by a framework. The framework is used for testing and hence called a *testing framework*. A testing framework makes a test case more efficient and robust. The framework includes features like handling test data, test standards, test repositories, page objects, and so forth.

Several Python frameworks can be used with Selenium. One of the most commonly used frameworks is unittest. The unittest framework, including its modules and functions, is described next.

The Unittest Framework

The unittest framework is a Python testing framework that is based on the XUnit framework design pattern developed by Kent Beck and Erich Gamma. It is also known as PyUnit. The unittest framework is commonly used to generate reports based on automated test cases.

In this framework, a test case is tested in small individual units (like functions, methods, class, etc.) that determine the correctness of the web element or web page tests. These tests are carried out in small chunks or units by defining classes as methods and using assert functions.

Before jumping into the code, you need to know the following components that the unittest framework supports.

- A **test fixture** executes one or more test cases and the related cleanup actions. Creating proxy or temporary databases, starting a process on a server, or creating new directories are some examples of a text fixture.

- In a **test case** module, small individual units are tested. These units are related to the web elements that are to be tested. The unittest framework contains a base class and the test cases that are used for creating new test cases.

- A **test suite** aggregates multiple test cases. It can also be a combination of test suites. The execution of a test suite is the same as a test case.

- A **test runner** helps to run all the test cases and their associated results. The runner can be integrated with interfaces, such as a graph, text, or a special value indicating return values from the test case.

- A **test report** is the generated result or output of a test case (i.e., whether it is passed or failed). The test case's execution time is arranged in a systematic way to generate the report. These details are summarized in a report for the client.

155

Test Case 2: Unittest

First, the unittest library needs to be downloaded using pip in Python. The unittest framework code has several instances that can be incorporated in a test case.

setUp()

The setUp() method initializes the setup that is required to run a test case. It runs at the beginning of the test case. The number of test cases determines the setUp() method to be executed. For example, if there are ten test cases, then the setUp() method is executed ten times before any test case. This method configures the initial stages of a test case, such as setting a web driver and its associated components.

```python
import unittest
from selenium import webdriver

class Test(unittest.TestCase):

        #setUp Class method
        def setUp(self):
                self.driver=webdriver.Firefox(executable_path=r'C:\Users\
                        ADMIN\Desktop\geckodriver.exe')
                print("Firefox Browser Opened")

        def test_apress(self):
                self.driver.get("https://apress.com")
                print("Apress")

        def test_google(self):
                self.driver.get("https://google.com")
                print("Google")

        def test_facebook(self):
                self.driver.get("https://facebook.com")
                print("Facebook")
```

```python
    def test_twitter(self):
            self.driver.get("https://twitter.com")
            print("Twitter")

if __name__ =="__main__":
        unittest.main()
```

The setUp() method is beneficial when there are multiple test cases for the same web application or web page. This reduces the initial configuration or setup that is required before a test.

tearDown()

The tearDown() method is executed after each test case is executed. It is a class method in unittest that is only stated once. It is executed for each test case available in the unittest program.

```python
import unittest
from selenium import webdriver

class Test(unittest.TestCase):
        def setUp(self):
                self.driver=webdriver.Firefox(executable_path=r'C:\Users\
                            ADMIN\Desktop\geckodriver.exe')
                print("Opened Firefox Browser")

        def test_apress(self):
                self.driver.get("https://apress.com")
                print("Apress")

        def tearDown(self):
                self.driver.quit()
                print("Quit Browser")

if __name__ =="__main__":
        unittest.main()
```

This method contains actions such as closing the web driver or browser, and logout or any closure action related to the test case. The tearDown() method is executed once the setUp() method is executed regardless of the test case results (i.e., pass/fail).

> **Note**   A test case can contain both the setUp() and tearDown() methods in the same test class in unittest.

setUpClass

setUpClass is a class in unittest that is executed before any `setUp` or `tearDown` functions or any test cases present in the same test class. A class that contains this method executes it only once, and it is passed as a single argument. `setUpClass` has a class known as `@classmethod` that is stated before the `setUp()` function.

```python
import unittest
from selenium import webdriver

#Class Setup
class Test(unittest.TestCase):

        @classmethod
        def setUpClass(suc):
                suc.driver=webdriver.Firefox(executable_path=r'C:\Users\
                        ADMIN\Desktop\geckodriver.exe')
                print("Open Browser using setUpClass method")

        def test_apress(self):
                self.driver.get("https://apress.com")
                print("Open Apress Site")
if __name__ =="__main__":
        unittest.main()
```

The `setUp()` function is not mandatory in `setUpClass`. If this class fails to execute, it raises an exception, and the test cases or `tearDown()` function in it do not execute.

tearDownClass

The `tearDownClass` class is executed after `setUpClass` and all related test cases that are present in the same test class. This class is executed once before exiting the program.

```
import unittest
from selenium import webdriver

#Class Setup
class Test(unittest.TestCase):

        @classmethod
        def setUpClass(suc):
                suc.driver=webdriver.Firefox(executable_path=r'C:\Users\
                        ADMIN\Desktop\geckodriver.exe')
        print("Open Browser using setUpClass method")

        def test_apress(self):
                self.driver.get("https://apress.com")
                print("Open Apress Site")

        @classmethod
        def tearDownClass(suc):
                suc.driver.quit()
                print("Close Browser using tearDownClass method")
if __name__ =="__main__":
        unittest.main()
```

You can use this method regardless of the setUpClass method.

An example of all the classes and functions is shown in the following simple test case.

setUpModuleandtearDownModule

There are two modules available in Python on Selenium. The execution of setUpModule takes place at the beginning, and the teardownModule execution is at the end. These two modules were recently added to the unittest framework.

```
import unittest
from selenium import webdriver

class Test(unittest.TestCase):
        #Class setup
```

```
        @classmethod
        def setUpClass(suc):
                suc.driver=webdriver.Firefox(executable_path=r'C:\Users\
                        ADMIN\Desktop\geckodriver.exe')
                print("Open Browser using setUpClass method")

        def setUp(self):
                print("Execute setUp")

        #test case
        def test_apress(self):
                self.driver.get("https://apress.com")
                print("Executing Test Case: Open Apress Site")
        def tearDown(self):
                print("Execute tearDown")

        @classmethod
        def tearDownClass(suc):
                suc.driver.quit()
                print("Close Browser using tearDownClass method")

        #Two Modules
        def setUpModule():
                print("Executes setUpModule")

        def tearDownModule():
                print("Executes tearDownModule")

if __name__ =="__main__":
        unittest.main()
```

In the program, the print statement in setUpModule() is printed first followed by setUpClass(), setUp(), test_apress(), tearDown(), tearDownClass(), and finally, tearDownModule() is printed.

Test Execution Order

Since there are different modules, classes, functions, and test cases defined, it is important to know the order of execution in the unittest framework. The execution order is determined by the priority given to the modules, classes, and functions, which are defined regardless of the positions in the program. The entire execution flow of a test case is shown in Figure 12-1.

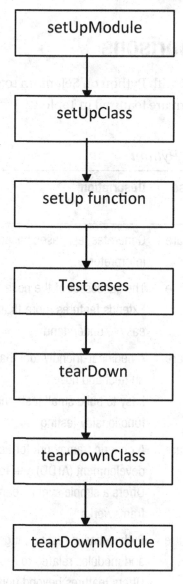

Figure 12-1. *Order of execution in unittest framework*

The order of execution for test cases is in alphabetical order by default in unittest. To prioritize, you can define the same name to all the test cases followed by a sequential number for each; for example, test1, test2, test3, test4, and so on.

Note   If there are multiple test cases, then they are executed in alphabetical order.

Testing Tool Comparisons

Many testing tools can be used with Python on Selenium to generate reports and test web applications. Some of them are featured in Table 12-1.

Table 12-1. *Testing Tools in Python*

Testing Tool	Category	License Type	Description
DocTest	Unit Testing	Freeware	Generates test cases based on the output of a Python interpreter
Nose2	Unit Testing	Freeware	The successor of the nose testing framework Extends features more than the nose framework; very easy to understand
Pytest	Unit Testing	Freeware	A beginner-friendly tool that supports integration with unittest and nose Easy to build small tests that can later scale to complex functionality testing
Robot	Acceptance Testing	Freeware	A generic framework for acceptance test-driven development (ATDD) and robotic process automation (RPA) Offers a simple syntax; easy to implement with other frameworks
Testify	Unit Testing	Freeware	Python-based testing plugin providing more functionality and modules related to reporting Offers features beyond unittest and nose

Summary

This final chapter explained the test cases intended to get the same results using different approaches. The unitttest framework is also used by Google to automate test cases. The framework is elaborated with basic terminologies and modules. Each module was examined with a testing example associated with it. When all the modules are combined in a single test case, the order of each module execution forms a flowing pattern. We wrapped up the chapter with a comparison of different testing tools supported by Python Selenium.

Correction to: Introduction to Selenium

Sujay Raghavendra

Correction to: Introduction to Selenium

Chapter 1 in: Sujay Raghavendra, *Python Testing with Selenium:* Learn to Implement Different Testing Techniques Using the Selenium WebDriver https://doi.org/10.1007/978-1-4842-6249-8

The original version of the chapter 1 was inadvertently published with the incomplete artwork for Figures 1-1 & 1-2 and the corrections have been incorporated in Chapter 1.

The updated online version of the chapter can be found at
https://doi.org/10.1007/978-1-4842-6249-8_1

© Sujay Raghavendra 2021
S. Raghavendra, *Python Testing with Selenium*, https://doi.org/10.1007/978-1-4842-6249-8_13

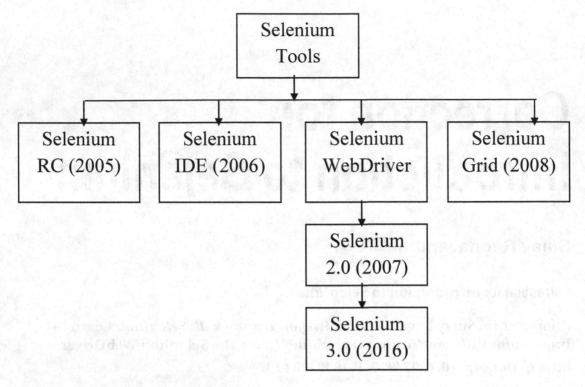

Figure 1-1. *Selenium suite*

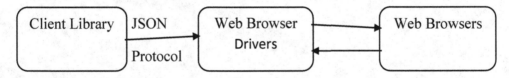

Figure 1-2. *Selenium WebDriver architecture*

Index

Printed in the United States
by Baker & Taylor Publisher Services